Praying the Dark Hours

Praying The Dark Hours

Jim Cotter

CANTERBURY
PRESS
Norwich

in association with
CAIRNS PUBLICATIONS

© Jim Cotter 1983, 1999, 2001 and 2011

This edition published in 2011 by the Canterbury Press Norwich
Editorial office
13–17 Long Lane,
London, EC1A 9PN, UK

in association with
CAIRNS PUBLICATIONS
Gernant, Aberdaron,
Pwllheli, Gwynedd, LL53 8BG
www.cottercairns.co.uk

Canterbury Press is an imprint of Hymns Ancient & Modern Ltd
(a registered charity)
13A Hellesdon Park Road, Norwich,
Norfolk, NR6 5DR, UK
www.canterburypress.co.uk

This book is a compilation of material previously published by Cairns
Publications in
Prayer at Night (1983), *Prayer at Night's Approaching* (2001), *Dazzling
Darkness* (1999), and *Waymarks* (2001)

British Library Cataloguing in Publication data

A catalogue record for this book is available
from the British Library

978 1 84825 109 0

Originated by The Manila Typesetting Company
Printed and bound by
CPI Group (UK) Ltd, Croydon, CR0 4YY

Contents

A thought for each night,
1 January to 31 December

WITH GRATITUDE

*to those unnamed and forgotten people
who have appreciated and commented upon this work
in conversations and in correspondence,*

*and to those without whose help and encouragement
a generation ago*
Prayer at Night *would never have found its way into
the public domain:
Jane of the Sisters of the Love of God in Oxford,
and Nadir of Karachi, London and Jersey,
both of whom are no longer with us,
and Esther of Rowlestone in Herefordshire,
and Ryder of London,*

*and to Alan Dodson,
who died in 2007,
whose typographical skills took Cairns Publications
from a clumsy hobby
to at least a modest professional enterprise,
and to Elin Dodson,
whose culinary skills have made every visit to Malvern
a mouth-watering delight,
to both of whom* Waymarks *was and is dedicated.*

Preface

The antecedents to this book go back nearly thirty years. Typed at home in Watford (albeit on an electric typewriter at the forefront of technology!) and photocopied at a shop in St Albans, *Prayer at Night* with *Cairns for the Journey* was first published in 1981 as little more than an A5 booklet with a blue cardboard cover. In time the two parts became two separate books, *Prayer at Night's Approaching* and *Waymarks*, both of them in pocket size and with reasonably large print. The former provided a form of night prayer on a weekly cycle, the latter a thought for the day throughout the year.

That original *Prayer at Night* and its subsequent editions have played a significant role in my life. Like most important things it was triggered by an incident which in itself carried no hint of what was to happen. It was the late 1970s and I was helping to tutor a course of training for public ministry in the Anglican diocese of St Albans. One Saturday evening we were praying, led by a student, the medieval office of Compline, though in a version in contemporary English, typical of the somewhat spare and flat liturgical prose of that generation. It occurred to me that we had addressed God as 'Lord' rather frequently – in fact, as I did a word count afterwards, 36 times in 12 minutes.

'Father' came second, used 12 times. All the other biblical images for God were either omitted or used rarely.

At the time I was beginning to realize that the prayer of the Christian Church had been slanted by a patriarchy and hierarchy of men who took nearly all the decisions and held nearly all the power. Rather than merely criticize, I was galvanized into attempting a variant. So *Prayer at Night* was born, with the intention of using a greater variety of both picture language and overall material than does the traditional order, yet retaining the same basic structure.

Like most writers of prayers, I was on a personal journey, trying to find words through which I could pray without reservations or questions getting in the way of the praying. (I relish such questioning and exploring, but not when I am attempting to turn my whole being Godwards with as much of that being as I am aware of.) So I am still moved to recall the response of one person who wrote to me saying that she could use the book at the end of a heavy day when her brain was hurting.

Of course none of the words here are meant to be set in stone. If you make alterations in the margin you are making your own contribution to the living prayer of God's people, not desecrating an ancient monument. I know that some people have been uncomfortable with the image of the 'unicorn' in Sunday's Thanksgiving. In fact, in earlier editions, the unicorn had a daily mention, but now the creature has to be content to be one of seven different images! But why the unicorn? It has been the question I have most frequently been asked by people who have used the book. Ah well, I reply, eyes half twinkling, 'You never know when you're going to meet one.' Slightly more seriously, they are like angels – you may find yourself entertaining them unawares. Like angels, too, they may bear messages from God. No one knows where they come from, nor how they reproduce. Perhaps they are beyond gender. They are rumoured in the ancient stories to be vibrant, alive, powerful creatures, yet also strangely pure and innocent. It has been said that only a 'virgin' can so attract unicorns that they come close enough for their wildness to be tamed. Some are depicted with a spiralling horn – symbol of the potential for integration, in each human being, of all that is apparently contradictory. And for medieval Europe the unicorn was a symbol for Christ, not least for that truth and freedom that are central to the Gospel. (PS to 'Puzzled of High Wycombe': please do not take any of this too solemnly. Play with the image of the unicorn. We don't have to *understand* everything. Why should we expect God always to make *sense?*)

Seriously, though it's doubtful if you will find a unicorn mentioned in the Bible (there is one verse where a one-horned creature is probably the rhinoceros), it is an image that is consonant with the heart of what is biblical. And the other images for that daily thanksgiving are: evening star (that comes from Aotearoa/New Zealand), snow leopard (a shy, elusive creature, well camouflaged, much as God so often seems to be), albatross (think of the steady beat of powerful wings), pilgrim staff, desert bread, and counsellor (the Holy Spirit in St John's Gospel).

A generation passes and a spiral makes one of its almost circular turns. In 2006 Cairns published a book of daily prayer, *Out of the Silence . . . Into the Silence*. Its format is mirrored in this book, its cousin – at least in the liturgical half, *Night by Night*. The layout on the page seeks to let the words breathe, with more space around them than is strictly necessary. The space hints at silence. Pauses are indicated to allow the prayer to be prayed through, not simply said.

The second half of the book is *Waymarks,* revisited and reshaped, a thought for each night of the year, but re-arranged so that each item is roughly the same length as each of the others. The aim has been to provide a contribution to the kind of question that rises within us in the often troubled silences and sleeplessness of the night hours.

The book's subtitle was *Cairns for a Journey.* The cairn, the heap of stones, marking the summit of a mountain, or a turning point on a forest trail, or a modest pile at frequent intervals on a track that is not easy to follow, is a powerful image, not least for those of us who find life a pilgrimage, a journey with questions, via many temporary inns, rather than a dwelling in one place with the ancestors' answers.

Now cairns are never so solid that they last for centuries. The stones can easily be scattered. Maybe you find yourself building one in your garden, to mark an event that no one but you remembers.

Sometimes you build a cairn from stones hewn from a quarry, under the harsh heat of midsummer. Boulders have been split, stones have been shaped, wheelbarrows have carried them. The cairn marks a place of deep and prolonged suffering and mutely says: this wisdom has been hard won.

Most of these waymarks are addressed to 'you'. This convention does not indicate the author speaking to the reader. Is the author being addressed by 'God', 'angel', 'friend', 'inner voice'? You, the reader, are invited to overhear, and to join in the conversation with your own pondering.

Jim Cotter
Aberdaron
June 2011

xii

Forewords

Foreword to the original edition of Prayer at Night

The Office of Compline is sometimes referred to as 'the goodnight prayer of the Church', with the implication that it is a sort of liturgical lullaby rounding off the day and designed to ensure a quiet night. This can be justified, as in the paraphrase of the psalm in these pages: 'I will lie down in peace and take my rest, for it is in God alone that I dwell unafraid.'

But praying at night involves considerably more than a peaceful passage through the hours of darkness. We 'let go' into sleep just as, one day, we shall have to 'let go' into death; and it is good to get accustomed to something of what that surrender involves. One of the prayers for Friday puts it acutely: 'give us courage to face what must decay, the disintegration of our mortal flesh, and give us faith to shed our false and deadly selves, to let them be as smoke vanishing in the evening breeze . . .'

The night hours are concerned with conflict as well as with quietness, and so preparation for them includes the armour of God for spiritual struggle and filling our minds with a range of strong biblical imagery in order to make a positive affirmation that God is Love. We also need to be ready to explore what this statement means in itself and what it demands from us – an exercise which will not necessarily lead to comfort or reassurance.

Prayer in the night is different from prayer in the day. Whether it is 'waiting for the dawn' in the early hours, or 'doing battle' with the 'powers of evil' in the middle of the night, it requires a naked exposure before God – the kind of nakedness that can be clothed in the daytime by those familiar distractions which make it more difficult to stay still and keep attentive to God. So a liturgical office that is a gateway into the night needs to take account of this fact. Here we are given a form of Compline which is sharp as well as consoling in its reality and relevance. Based on the traditional pattern, it stands on its own, but could equally well fit into the daily cycle of the parochial or monastic office. The whole has undoubtedly emerged from the prayed experience of the compiler, and so evokes a similar response in the user.

For example, the confessions (or 'recognitions'), different for each day of the week, taken together do not let us get away with the meaningless mutter that can, in the familiar formula, all too easily pass for penitence. Because on Friday and Saturday we spell out our nastiness and face its effect on other people, and we see just how our personal indifference and carelessness react negatively within the whole of creation, the more traditional phraseology of previous evenings comes alive, and the words have their intended impact. The choice of psalms and the subtlety of the paraphrasing, both encourage and challenge us. There is a lot here about light piercing darkness, about mercy and forgiveness, about trust in God; above all, there is praise, worship, awe in face of the Creator of 'the ever-changing hills'. God is our refuge and strength, and gives us gifts even while we sleep, but also the inescapable, all-knowing fashioner of 'cell and tissue, blood and bone', who searches us out and holds us, as in the palm of a hand.

Prayer at Night is authentic because in it the wisdom of the centuries, in scripture and above all in the psalms, is filled out with contemporary Christian experience of God as 'Life-giver, Pain-bearer, Love-maker' – a phrase that makes us think of what we mean when we use the more familiar trinitarian formula – and the awareness that each of us who tries to pray is part of the human whole, subject to all manner of powers of darkness, including of course the ever-present threat of nuclear extinction.

So we are taken over the threshold from daytime, not in a holy huddle of 'me, myself, and God', but, whether prayed alone or in company, as representatives of humanity, acknowledging creaturehood before God – but also humbly grateful for our partnership with God in that loving work of redemption which 'pours out lifeblood in love for us', and indeed asks the same of us.

Jane SLG
Oxford, 1983

This was originally written when Jane was serving as Mother General of the Sisters of the Love of God, an Anglican contemplative community in Oxford. She died on St Patrick's Day in 1995, having with her sisters prayed much during the hours of darkness – their night office is at 2 a.m. – she can now perhaps be appreciated as the patron saint of all those who seek to pray in the dark hours and in their own dark places.

Foreword to the original edition of Waymarks

'You only need waymarks in a fog,' said a friend. I reassured him that it feels as if my life has been lived in a 'cloud of unknowing', and I have always treasured the cairns and markers that have helped me to continue my spiritual pilgrimage.

Jim Cotter has been a personal waymark for me over the last twelve years, and his writing for longer than that. This collection reflects his own journey: his wrestling with his own humanity and sexuality, his trinitarian God, his 'brainsquall' – and even his need of a bishop! (See 4 August.) As with much of Jim's writing I have found that these cairns can be used for both personal and corporate meditation. I have already discovered my purple passages in this book, which I shall turn to regularly for the rest of my life and which I shall want to share with others.

Waymarks connects for me with the bustle and rhythms of Manchester and with the beauty and solitude of Llandecwyn in North Wales, where Jim now spends part of the year. They help to guide me through the fog in city and on mountain top.

Stephen Lowe
Bishop of Hulme
Manchester, February 2001

How To Use The Prayer, Night By Night

Some practical suggestions

Think 'simplicity' and think 'silence'. The prayers are neither complicated nor long. The lines are mostly laid out so that each can be said comfortably on one breath, and a pause taken between the lines. The words on the page are surrounded with empty space so that they can breathe. Do not hurry. Pause often. Wait until a sentence or section or prayer has ended – and only then turn the page. Choose an uncluttered place in which to pray. Keep to one posture to encourage your bodily self to be still. Let your backbone be straight – even if you are horizontal!

Night by Night has four sections:

The *first* provides all that is needed for each night of the week, but you may sometimes wish to use material from the other three sections. Turn to the day of the week. The sequence of the prayer is this:

•	Invocation	Opening yourself to God
•	Thanksgiving	Being glad about . . .
•	Recognition	Being sorry about . . .

- Psalm(s) Praising and praying
            with our ancestors
- Reading Listening to the Bible
- Hymn   Joining ancient and modern
            voices
- Prayers Various

The *second* section provides material for special seasons and occasions (you may wish to add your own), as variants for the everyday readings and antiphons to the Nunc Dimittis: Advent, Christmas, Epiphany, Lent, Passiontide, Easter, Ascension, Pentecost, Trinity, saints' days, the departed.

The *third* section is for particular prayers, for people and concerns close to your own heart.

The *fourth* section is for occasional use. Here are prayers of blessing, one looking outwards to city and world, one focusing on your own body. There is a meditative prayer concerned with all that rises to trouble and disturb us, often and especially during the night. There is a litany so that you can bring to heart and mind those in the city who are awake while others sleep. And there are prayers of surrender and covenant.

The typography is designed to guide you:

CENTERED ITALICS indicate a new subdivision.
Bold letters indicate 'everybody joins in'.
Ordinary letters indicate the leader's part.
If you are praying on your own, simply ignore the
  difference between the last two.
Three dots like this . . . suggest taking time to pause.

Square brackets like this [ ] indicate the kind of prayer appropriate, but you have to supply your own words.

If you fall silent at any point, and you remain silent for the rest of the time you have put aside for the prayer, do not feel guilty about ending and not getting through all the words. Quality matters more than quantity! And, come to think of it, there may still be chores to do before going to bed. And these can also be made part of our praying in the dark hours.

Sources And Acknowledgements

Some of the material is more or less the same for each night of the week. The first section of the *Invocation* is traditional, adapted by the compiler. The second section varies, but each is a quotation from the Bible:

Sunday	1 Peter 5.8
Monday	Isaiah 40.31
Tuesday	John 4.24
Wednesday	1 Corinthians 16.13–14
Thursday	Ephesians 6.18
Friday	Matthew 26.40–41
Saturday	Psalm 127.2

The third section is Psalm 121.1.

The *Thanksgiving* is almost the same each night of the week and is by the compiler. The prayers of *Recognition* are mostly by the compiler but draw extensively on biblical sources. I know that the first prayers for Tuesday, Friday and Saturday were written by others, but I have lost track of them. I apologize if I have infringed copyright, and I am always willing to make reasonable amends. The prayer for Wednesday could be given the title, 'The Five New Testament Commandments'.

The second of the prayers for Saturday is a re-working of the Collect for Purity at the beginning of the service of Holy Communion in the Book of Common Prayer.

The *Psalms* are as follows:

Sunday	Psalm 103.1–18, followed by a coda with New Testament themes, by the compiler
Monday	Psalms 134; 4; 23
Tuesday	Psalms 121; 16.7–11; 31.1–5
Wednesday	Psalm 139.1–18
Thursday	Psalms 46; 91.1–5; 11.14–16
Friday	Psalms 130; 126
Saturday	Psalms 42; 43

The *Readings* are:

Sunday	Paraphrases of the first four of the Beatitudes from Matthew 5
Monday	Paraphrases of the last four of the Beatitudes from Matthew 5
Tuesday	Galatians 5.22–23; Luke 6.27–28, 35–38; Matthew 6.31–34; John 4.34
Wednesday	1 John 4.18–20; Jeremiah 14.9; 2 Corinthians 4.6–11; Ephesians 3.16–19
Thursday	John 4.14; 2 Timothy 1.7; John 15.4; 14.27; 1 Thessalonians 5.24
Friday	John 15.12–13; Romans 8.14–17; Romans 8.19–23; Romans 8.38–39
Saturday	1 Timothy 6.6–8; 10; 11; Proverbs 31.8–9; 2 Corinthians 4.16–18; Isaiah 61.1–2

The *Readings* for the 29th, 30th and 31st of the month are:

Sunday	Unfolding of Isaiah 30.15
Monday	Hosea 11.8–9
Tuesday	Isaiah 45.6–7
Wednesday	Amos 5.24
Thursday	Ruth 2.16–17
Friday	Micah 6.6–8
Saturday	Hosea 2.14

The *Hymns* are:

Sunday	Compiler's version of the hymn written before the fourth century, 'Phos hilarion'.
Monday	Thomas Ken's hymn, adapted by compiler.
Tuesday	A hymn by Brian Wren, from his collection, *Bring Many Names*, printed here by permission of Stainer and Bell Ltd © 1989 for the world except USA, Canada, Australia, New Zealand.
Wednesday	An old Latin hymn, J. M. Neale's translation, adapted by compiler.
Thursday	Mrs C. F. Alexander's version of 'St Patrick's Breastplate', slightly adapted by compiler.
Friday	By Charles Wesley.
Saturday	By compiler; may be sung to the tune 'The Ash Grove'.

The *Prayers* are:

'Into your hands' is from the Psalms, adapted.
'Antiphon' and 'Nunc Dimittis': the Antiphon and the

Nunc Dimittis resonate with Luke 2.29–32.

There are three versions of the 'Lord's Prayer', two by compiler, the one for Friday inspired by Louis Evely's book, *Our Father.*

'I will lie down in peace': the first two lines are from the Psalms, the last four by compiler.

More specifically,

Sunday	'Praying with Mary' and 'For this house' are by compiler; the Blessing is traditional.
Monday	'For the blessing of touch' is by compiler; 'For joy' comes from a source I haven't been able to trace; the Blessing is by compiler, but owes the phrase 'dazzling darkness' to Henry Vaughan.
Tuesday	'For peace' is the prayer for world peace written by Satish Kumar; 'For refreshment' is from the traditional version of Compline, slightly adapted by compiler; the Blessing, I think, comes from William Temple.
Wednesday	'For our work' is slightly adapted by compiler from a prayer by the great scholar of Chinese history, Joseph Needham; the 'greeting to our ancestors is by compiler; the Blessing is from 2 Corinthians 13.14.
Thursday	'For inner peace' is from the Book of Common Prayer; 'For the unity of humankind' is from a prayer written for an inter-faith gathering; the Blessing is by compiler.

Friday   'Christ crucified' is by compiler; 'Lighten
                our darkness' is from the Book of
                Common Prayer, adapted by compiler;
                the Blessing is by compiler.
Saturday   Both 'Loving God' and 'Abiding and
                increasing' are prayers adapted from
                two in the Book of Common Prayer; the
                Blessing is by compiler.

The *Readings and Antiphons for special days and seasons*
are:

Advent   Isaiah 40.3–5; traditional
Christmas   John 1.14, paraphrased by compiler;
                John 1.14
Epiphany   Luke 2.30–32; Psalm 86.9
Lent   Isaiah 58.6–8; John 17.19
Passiontide   Hosea 6.1–2; Philippians 2.7
Easter   1 Corinthians 15.20–22; Easter Greeting
Ascension   Based on Colossians 2.15; based on
                Hebrews 12.2
Pentecost   Romans 5.5 and 2 Timothy 1.7; John
                16.13
Trinity   Revelation 4.8 and 7.12; compiler, owing
                the line, 'Lover, Beloved, Mutual Friend'
                to Brian Wren, op. cit.
Saints' Days   Revelation 1.7–18 and 2.7, 10, 17; based
                on Revelation 5
The Departed   Alternative Service Book 1980; Russian
                Kontakion

Additional Prayers are:

'In the life of the city at night' by compiler, 1989,
inspired by the view of the city of Sheffield from the
chapel at the top of his house.

'God be . . .' is an extended, full-body version by
compiler of the traditional prayer, 'God be in my head'.

'To the troubling unknown' by compiler.

'The fauna of the night' by compiler; this owes much
to W. H. Auden's poem honouring Sigmund Freud; the
section 'Encounter them' is based on the story of
Jacob's struggle with the 'stranger' in Genesis
32.22–32; 'robed as destinies' is a phrase of Philip
Larkin's in his poem 'Churchgoing'.

'Dark angels' by compiler. This owes much to R. M.
Rilke's words in his *Letters to a Young Poet* (Norton,
New York, revised edition, 1974).

'The warming of fear' by compiler. I read of
'smoke-self' and 'flame-self' somewhere in the writings
of Thomas Merton.

'A prayer of surrender' is based on one by Charles de
Foucauld.

The three covenant prayers are by the compiler.

The prayer for 'friends, here and beyond' is based on
one by John V. Taylor, whose inspiration for this and
much else is gratefully acknowledged.

NIGHT BY NIGHT

SUNDAY

Invocation

The angels of God guard us through the night,
and quieten the powers of darkness.
The Spirit of God be our guide
to lead us to peace and to glory.

People of God, be sober, be watchful;
your adversary the devil as a roaring lion prowls about,
seeking someone to devour:
whom withstand, steadfast in the faith.

Our help is in the name of the eternal God,
who is making the heavens and the earth.

Thanksgiving

Dear God, thank you for all that is good,
for our creation and our humanity,
for the stewardship you have given us of this planet earth,
for the gifts of life and of one another,

for the people and events of this day . . .

for friends and families . . .

for your love, unbounded and eternal . . .

O Thou, most holy and beloved,
my companion, my unicorn, my guide upon the way.

Recognition

We have injured your love:
Binder of wounds, heal us.
We stumble in the darkness:
Light of the world, guide us.
We forget that we are your home:
Spirit of God, dwell in us . . .

God of joy, we rejoice in you.

You run to meet us like a welcoming friend,
you laugh with us in the merriment of heaven,
you feast with us at the great banquet,
Clown of clowns, Fool of fools,
the only Entertainer of jesters.

God of joy, we rejoice in you.

Psalms

Eternal Spirit, flow through our being and open our lips
that our mouths may proclaim your praise.
Let us worship the God of love:
Alleluia. Alleluia.

There is no end to your mercy,
enduring and infinite is your love.
There is no end to your mercy,
enduring and infinite is your love.

From the deep places of my soul I praise you, O God:
I lift up my heart and glorify your holy name.
From the deep places of my soul I praise you, O God;
how can I forget all your goodness towards me?
You forgive all my sin, you heal all my weakness,
you rescue me from the brink of disaster,
you crown me with mercy and compassion.
You satisfy my being with good things,
so that my youth is renewed like an eagle's.
You fulfil all that you promise,
justice for all the oppressed.
You made known your ways to Moses,
and all the people saw your deeds.
You are full of forgiveness and grace,
endlessly patient, faithful in love.
You do not haunt us with our sins,
nor nurse grievances against us.
You do not repay evil with evil,
for you are greater than our sins.
As vast as the heavens are in comparison with the earth,
so great is your love to those who trust you.
As far as the east is from the west,
so far do you fling our sins from us.
Just as parents are merciful to their children,
so are you merciful and kind towards us.
For you know how fragile we are,
that we are made of the dust of the earth.

Our days are like the grass,
they bloom like the flowers of the field:
the wind blows over them and they are gone,
and no one can tell where they stood.
Only your merciful goodness endures;
age after age you act justly
towards all who hold on to your covenant,
who take your words to heart and fulfil them.

There is no end to your mercy,
enduring and infinite is your love.
There is no end to your mercy,
enduring and infinite is your love.

Silence

For you have triumphed over the power of death,
and draw us to your presence with songs of joy.
We hear the echo of your angels praising you,
and the whole communion of your saints,
those who have walked in your narrow ways,
and heard the voice of your yearning,
whose food is to do your will,
and in whom you take great delight.
From the widest bounds of the universe
to the depths of my very being
the whispers and cries of joy
vibrate to a shining glory,
O God, our beginning and our end.

There is no end to your mercy,
enduring and infinite is your love.
There is no end to your mercy,
enduring and infinite is your love.

Reading

First Sunday of the month
Poverty

Blighted are those who crave more and more possessions:

they will be crushed by the weight and burden of them.

Pause

Blessed are those who are ready to do without,
to be empty, to be nothing,
to be humble and open to receive,
knowing their need of God:

they have found the secret of living,
and are rich indeed.

Second Sunday of the month
Grief

Blighted are those who wallow in self-pity:

they will sink into bitterness and despair.

Pause

Blessed are those who accept their experience of sorrow:

they will grow in courage and compassion.

Third Sunday of the month
Struggle

Blighted are those who have ceased to care and be disturbed,
and are now too much at ease:

they will be bored
and they will disintegrate into dust.

Pause

Blessed are those who hunger and thirst and strive
for what is just and good:

they will be made whole,
and will be well content.

Fourth Sunday of the month
Security

Blighted are those who, in their insecurity,
look anxiously for appreciation from others:

they claim everything for themselves,
and yet possess nothing,
wandering unhappily
and belonging nowhere.

Pause

Blessed are those who have accepted their insecurity,
and are content to go unrecognized and unrewarded,
claiming nothing for themselves:

the freedom of the earth is theirs;
never exiled, they are everywhere at home.

29th, 30th and 31st of the month

Gently turning again, I breathe more freely.
Quietly waiting and trusting, my inner strength grows.

Hymn

Hail, gladdening Light, of God's pure glory poured,
who is the great Creator, heavenly, blest,
holiest of holies, Jesus Christ who reigns.

Now we are come to the sun's hour of rest,
the lights of evening round us shine;
we hymn the God of love, eternal Spirit divine.

You are worthy, O God, at all times to be sung,
with clear and truthful voice:
light of light, giver of life, alone!
Therefore in all the world your glories, Christ, we own.

Into your hands

Living God, faithful and trustworthy,
delighting in me, yearning for me,
into your hands I cast the whole of my being,
for you are transforming me, bodily, spiritually.
Keep me, dear God, as the apple of your eye,
enfold me under the shadow of your wings.

Antiphon to the Nunc Dimittis

Inspire me while waking,
restore me while sleeping,
that awake in the night I may watch with Christ,
and asleep may rest in your peace.

An unfolding of the Nunc Dimittis

I give you thanks, Beloved,
I have lived to see this day.
Your promise is fulfilled,
and my duty done.
Each night you give me your peace,
for I have glimpsed with my own eyes
the liberation you prepare for all people,
a light to the world in its darkness,
and the glory of all who serve your love.
I give you thanks, Beloved,
for ceaselessly you are giving us life,
bearing our pain, and making love with us,
this night and always.

Praying in Christ

Eternal Spirit,
Life-giver, Pain-bearer, Love-maker,
source of all that is and that shall be,
Father and Mother of us all,
loving God, in whom is heaven:

The hallowing of your name
echo through the universe.
The way of your justice
be followed by the peoples of the world.
Your heavenly will
be done by all created beings.
Your commonwealth of peace and freedom
sustain our hope and come on earth.

With the bread we need for today,
feed us.
In the hurts we absorb from one another,
forgive us.
In times of temptation and test,
strengthen us.
From trials too severe to endure,
spare us.
From the grip of all that is evil,
free us.

For you reign in the glory
of the power that is love,
now and for ever. Amen.

I will lie down in peace

I will lie down in peace and take my rest,
for it is in you alone that I dwell unafraid.
I embrace you, Life-giver, Pain-bearer, Love-maker,
I love you and adore you above all for ever.
May your name be revered beyond the furthest star,
delighted in and glorified above all for ever.

[Particular Prayers]

Praying with Mary

Rejoicing with you,
grieving with you,
Mary, graced by God –
Love's mystery did come to you –
of our race we deem you most the blessed,
save but the blessed One,
the child who came to birth in you.
Woman holy,
trembling at the presence of the angel,
willing the rare and marvellous exchange,
in the darkness holding the Unseen,
bearing forth the word made flesh for earth's redeeming,
take to your heart our world,
and pray for humankind,
that we with you be bearers of the Christ,
through this and all our days,
and at the last.

For this house

Be present, living Christ, within us,
your dwelling place and home,
that this house may be one
where our darkness is penetrated by your light,
where our troubles are calmed by your peace,
where our evil is redeemed by your love,
where our pain is transformed in your suffering,
and where our dying is glorified in your risen life.

Blessing

God of love and mercy,
give to us and all your people
rest and peace.

The divine Spirit dwells in us:
Thanks be to God.

MONDAY

Invocation

The angels of God guard us through the night,
and quieten the powers of darkness.
The Spirit of God be our guide
to lead us to peace and to glory.

They that wait for the Spirit shall renew their strength:
they shall mount up with wings as eagles,
they shall run and not be weary,
they shall walk and not faint.

Our help is in the name of the eternal God,
who is making the heavens and the earth.

Thanksgiving

Dear God, thank you for all that is good,
for our creation and our humanity,
for the stewardship you have given us of this planet earth,
for the gifts of life and of one another,

for the people and events of this day . . .

for all with whom we have to do in our communities . . .

for your love, unbounded and eternal . . .

O Thou, most holy and beloved,
my companion, my evening star, my guide upon the way.

Recognition

We grieve and confess
that we harm and have been harmed,
to the third and fourth generations,
that we are so afraid of pain
that we shield ourselves from being vulnerable to others,
and refuse to be open and trusting as a child . . .

God of wholeness, we rest in you.

You listen with us to the sound of running water,
you sit with us under the shade of the trees of our healing,
you walk once more with us in the garden in the cool of
    the day,
the oil of your anointing penetrates the cells of our being,
the warmth of your hands steadies us and gives us courage.

God of wholeness, we rest in you.

Psalms

Eternal Spirit, flow through our being and open our lips
that our mouths may proclaim your praise.
Let us worship the God of love:
Alleluia. Alleluia.

We your servants bless you, dear God,
as we stand by night in your house.
We lift up our hands towards the holy place,
and give you thanks and praise.
Bless us from all places where you dwell,
O God, Creator of heaven and earth.
We your servants bless you, dear God,
as we stand by night in your house.

Silence

Our hearts are awry: can we believe
that all will come right in the end?
Our hearts are awry: can we believe
that all will come right in the end?

Answer me when I call, O God,
for you are the God of justice.
You set me free when I was hard-pressed:
be gracious to me now, for you hear my prayer.
How long will I shun your glory and shame you?
How long will I love what is worthless and run after lies?
You have shown me such wonderful kindness.
When I call out in prayer you hear me.
Let me tremble, admit defeat, and sin no more.
Let me look deep into my heart before I sleep, and be still.

I bring my gifts, just as I am,
and put my trust in you, my God.
Many are asking: 'Who can make us content?
The light of your countenance has gone from us, O God.'
Yet you have given my heart more gladness
than those whose corn and wine and oil increase.
I lie down in peace and sleep comes at once,
for in you alone, O God, do I dwell unafraid.

Our hearts are awry: can we believe
that all will come right in the end?
Our hearts are awry: can we believe
that all will come right in the end?

Silence

Dwell in me that I may dwell in you.
Dwell in me that I may dwell in you.

Dear God, you sustain me and feed me:
like a shepherd you guide me.
You lead me to an oasis of green,
to lie down by restful waters.
Quenching my thirst, you restore my life:
renewed and refreshed, I follow you,
a journey on the narrowest of paths.
Even when cliffs loom out of the mist,
my step is steady because of my trust.
Even when I go through the deepest valley,
with the shadow of darkness and death,
I shall fear no evil or harm.
For you are with me to give me strength,
your crook, your staff, at my side.

Even in the midst of my troubles,
with the murmurs of those who disturb me,
I know I can feast in your presence.
You spread a banquet before me,
you anoint my head with oil,
you stoop to wash my feet,
you fill my cup to the brim.
Your loving kindness and mercy
will meet me every day of my life.
By your Spirit you dwell within me,
and in the whole world around me,
and I shall abide in your house,
content in your presence for ever.

Dwell in me that I may dwell in you.
Dwell in me that I may dwell in you.

Reading

First Monday of the month
Love

Blighted are those who show no compassion
and are insensitive to the needs of others:

they will always complain of being misunderstood,
and they will never be loved.

Pause

Blessed are those who accept and forgive those who hurt
them:

they will find understanding and love.

Second Monday of the month
Truth

Blighted are those who live in delusion and fantasy:

they will be utterly lost.

Pause

Blessed are those who are honest with themselves,
who are being refined and chastened,
and seek to live the truth:

they will know themselves
and they will know God.

Third Monday of the month
Peace

Blighted are those who are at war with themselves,
who spread evil and division and hatred,
seeking to dominate others;

they breed their own downfall,
and they never know trust and friendship.

Pause

Blessed are those who create reconciliation and goodwill
    wherever they go,
returning good for evil:

they are indeed the friends of God.

Fourth Monday of the month
Life

Blighted are those whose lives are shallow and full of fear,
who cannot respond in truth when they are challenged:

they will freeze in death.

Pause

Blessed are those who shed their pettiness,
and know the deep things of God and of themselves,
and so persevere at whatever the cost –
insult, slander, exile, death:

they will have life
and know it abundantly.

29th, 30th and 31st of the month

A change of heart moves me, tenderness kindles within me. I
shall not let loose with fury, or come to you with threats. For
I am God, and not mortal: I am the Holy One in your midst.

Hymn

**Glory to you, my God, this night,
for all the blessings of the light,
to you, from whom all good does come,
our life, our health, our lasting home.**

Teach me to live, that I may dread
the grave as little as my bed.
Teach me to die, that so I may
rise glorious at the awful day.

O may I now on you repose,
and may kind sleep my eyelids close,
sleep that may me more vigorous make
to serve my God when I awake.

If I lie restless on my bed,
your word of healing peace be said.
If powerful dreams rise in the night,
transform their darkness into light.

All praise to God, sustaining us,
redeeming and transfiguring us,
thanksgiving in eternity,
all praise, beloved Trinity.

Into your hands

Living God, faithful and trustworthy,
delighting in me, yearning for me,
into your hands I cast the whole of my being,
for you are transforming me, bodily, spiritually.
Keep me, dear God, as the apple of your eye,
enfold me under the shadow of your wings.

Antiphon to the Nunc Dimittis

Inspire me while waking,
restore me while sleeping,
that awake in the night I may watch with Christ,
and asleep may rest in your peace.

An unfolding of the Nunc Dimittis

I give you thanks, Beloved,
I have lived to see this day.
Your promise is fulfilled,
and my duty done.
Each night you give me your peace,
for I have glimpsed with my own eyes
the liberation you prepare for all people,
a light to the world in its darkness,
and the glory of all who serve your love.
I give you thanks, Beloved,
for ceaselessly you are giving us life,
bearing our pain, and making love with us,
this night and always.

Praying in Christ

Abba, **our Father,**
Amma, **our Mother,**
Beloved, **our God,**
Creator of all:
your name be held holy,
your domain spread among us,
your wisdom be our guide,

your way be our path,
your will be done well,
at all times, in all places,
on earth as in heaven.
Give us the bread
we need for today,
the manna of your promise,
the taste of your tomorrow.
As we release those
indebted to us,
so forgive us our debts,
our trespass on others.
Fill us with courage
in time of our testing.
Spare us from trials
too severe to endure.
Free us from the grip
of the powers that bind.
For yours is the goodness
in which evil dissolves;
yours is the joy
that sounds through the pain;
yours is the life
which swallows up death.
Yours is the glory,
the transfiguring light,
the victory of love,
for time and eternity,
for age after age.
So be it. Amen.

I will lie down in peace

I will lie down in peace and take my rest,
for it is in you alone that I dwell unafraid.
I embrace you, Life-giver, Pain-bearer, Love-maker,
I love you and adore you above all for ever.
May your name be revered beyond the furthest star,
delighted in and glorified above all for ever.

[Particular Prayers]

For the blessing of touch

Giver of life, Bearer of pain, Maker of love,
affirming in your incarnation the goodness of the flesh,
may the yearnings of our bodies
be fulfilled in sacraments of love,
and our earthly embracings
a foretaste of the pleasure that shall be,
in the glory of the resurrection body of Jesus Christ.

For joy

Dear God,
the Source of the whole world's gladness
and the Bearer of its pain,
may your unconquerable joy
rest at the heart of all our trouble and distress.

Blessing

Friend and Lover,
bless us and keep us.
Light of the world,
shine on our faces.
Transfigured Yeshua,
lift us to glory.
May the darkness of night
deepen and dazzle.

The divine Spirit dwells in us:
Thanks be to God.

TUESDAY

Invocation

The angels of God guard us through the night,
and quieten the powers of darkness.
The Spirit of God be our guide
to lead us to peace and to glory.

God is spirit and those who worship God
must worship in spirit and in truth.

Our help is in the name of the eternal God,
who is making the heavens and the earth.

Thanksgiving

Dear God, thank you for all that is good,
for our creation and our humanity,
for the stewardship you have given us of this planet earth,
for the gifts of life and of one another,

for the people and events of this day . . .

for this neighbourhood/village/town/city . . .

for your love, unbounded and eternal . . .

O Thou, most holy and beloved,
my companion, my snow leopard, my guide upon the way.

Recognition

Merciful God,
we have not loved you with our whole heart,
nor our neighbours as ourselves.
Forgive what we have been,
accept us as we are,
and guide what we shall be ...

God of mercy, we thank you.

You forgive our past sin,
you bless us abundantly,
you give us new strength,
you fill us with gratitude,
you sow in us seeds of new life,
you shape us for glory.

God of mercy, we thank you.

Psalms

Eternal Spirit, flow through our being and open our lips
that our mouths may proclaim your praise.
Let us worship the God of love:
Alleluia. Alleluia.

Companion on my journey, protector at my side,
I venture on the way in simple, childlike trust.

Companion on my journey, protector at my side,
I venture on the way in simple, childlike trust.

I look towards the mountain ranges,
and fear their lurking terrors.
The pilgrim path takes me through them,
by rocks and ravines, ambush and vultures.
Stormy winds swirl round the summits,
avalanches threaten across trackless screes.
The hills themselves give no courage or strength,
and I turn once again to my God.
Tempted to slide back into mud,
down to the bliss of oblivion,
yet I hear the lure of my lover,
whispering through my story's confusion.
The God who draws me is urging me on,
and I discover my faltering Yes.
I stumble along the rough pathways,
surprised by a hand that is grasping my own.
To and fro, back and forth,
on the twists of the journey,
courage moves me onwards,
faith trusts in the future;
wisdom makes me pause,
I rest by the stream;
taking time to delve deep,
I listen for a voice.

Companion on my journey, protector at my side,
I venture on the way in simple, childlike trust.
Companion on my journey, protector at my side,
I venture on the way in simple, childlike trust.

Pause

I reach for the unknown mountain,
to the summit where God speaks anew,
on the boundary of earth and heaven,
the frontier of time and eternity,
the place of a special revealing,
marked by the stones of a cairn.
As I ponder the codes of my dreaming,
I am surprised by the mystery of God.
The hills themselves slowly change,
never as firm as they seem;
shrouded, brooding, and dark,
their rocks splintered by frost,
worn away by the lashing of storms,
no strength in themselves to support me,
only from God comes my help.
With the wind of the Spirit empower me,
stirring the substance of earth,
moving my innermost being,
yet keeping me from all lasting harm.
Keep watch, do not slumber, guardian of your people,
shade from the heat, healer and guide.
Nourish the life of my truest self,
from this moment on and for ever.

Companion on my journey, protector at my side,
I venture on the way in simple, childlike trust.
Companion on my journey, protector at my side,
I venture on the way in simple, childlike trust.

Silence

Greet us all in the joy of your presence.
Greet us all in the joy of your presence.

We give you thanks for the wisdom of your counsel,
even at night you have instructed our hearts.
In the silence of the darkest of hours
we open our ears to the whisper of your voice.
We have set your face always before us,
in every cell of our being you are there.
As we tremble on the narrowest of paths,
the steadying of your hand gives us courage.
Fleet of foot, with our eyes on the goal,
headlong in the chasm we shall not fall.
Therefore our hearts rejoice and our spirits are glad,
our whole being will rest secure.
For you will not give us over to the power of death,
nor let your faithful ones see the pit.
You will show us the path of life:
in your countenance is the fullness of joy.
From the spring of your heart flow rivers of delight,
a fountain of water that shall never run dry.

Greet us all in the joy of your presence.
Greet us all in the joy of your presence.

Silence

In the midst of struggle and pain
we trust in the love that endures.
In the midst of struggle and pain
we trust in the love that endures.

I am bowed down by the heat of battle;
exhausted I limp back to my tent.
Here is my shelter, my refuge,
the place where I know God is with me.
Deliver me, rescue me, redeem me,
for you are just, and swift to save.
You are a stream of refreshment, an oasis of shade;
you give me manna in the wilderness, ever drawing me on.
Lead me and guide me for the sake of your name:
deliver me out of the nets that entangle me,
for you alone are my strength.
Into your hands I cast my whole being,
knowing that you will redeem me,
O God of salvation and truth.

In the midst of struggle and pain
we trust in the love that endures.
In the midst of struggle and pain
we trust in the love that endures.

Reading

First Tuesday of the month

The fruit of the Spirit is
love, joy, peace,
patience, kindness, goodness,
faithfulness, gentleness, self-discipline . . .

If we live by the Spirit,
let us also walk by the Spirit . . .

and bear one another's burdens,
and so fulfil the law of Christ . . .

Second Tuesday of the month

Love your enemies . . .

Do good to those who hate you . . .
Bless those who curse you . . .
Pray for those who abuse you . . .

Do good and lend, expecting nothing in return . . .

For God is kind to the ungrateful and selfish . . .

Be merciful as your Father is merciful . . .
Judge not and you will not be judged . . .
Condemn not and you will not be condemned . . .
Forgive and you will be forgiven . . .
Give, and it will be given to you . . .

For the measure you give will be the measure you receive . . .

Third Tuesday of the month

Do not ask anxiously,
What are we to eat?
What are we to drink?
What shall we wear? . . .

Set your heart and mind on God's commonwealth first,
and all the rest will come to you as well . . .

So do not be anxious about tomorrow.
Today has enough problems of its own.
Tomorrow can look after itself . . .

Fourth Tuesday of the month

My food is to do the will of the One who sent me,
to accomplish God's work . . .

I have food to eat of which you do not know . . .

29th, 30th and 31st of the month

I am the Living One, and there is none other:
I make the light, I create the darkness;
author alike of wellbeing and woe,
I, the Living One, do all these things.

Hymn

How wonderful the Three-in-One,
whose energies of dancing light
are undivided, pure, and good,
communing love in shared delight.

Before the flow of dawn and dark,
creation's Lover dreamed of earth,
and with a caring deep and wise
all things conceived and brought to birth.

The Lover's own Belov'd, in time,
between a cradle and a cross,
at home in flesh, gave love and life
to heal our brokenness and loss.

Their Equal Friend all life sustains
with greening power and loving care,
and calls us, born again by grace,
in Love's communing life to share.

How wonderful the living God:
Divine Belov'd, Empow'ring Friend,
Eternal Lover, Three-in-One,
our hope's beginning, way, and end.

Into your hands

Living God, faithful and trustworthy,
delighting in me, yearning for me,
into your hands I cast the whole of my being,
for you are transforming me, bodily, spiritually.
Keep me, dear God, as the apple of your eye,
enfold me under the shadow of your wings.

Antiphon to the Nunc Dimittis

Inspire me while waking,
restore me while sleeping,
that awake in the night I may watch with Christ,
and asleep may rest in your peace.

An unfolding of the Nunc Dimittis

I give you thanks, Beloved,
I have lived to see this day.
Your promise is fulfilled,
and my duty done.

34

Each night you give me your peace,
for I have glimpsed with my own eyes
the liberation you prepare for all people,
a light to the world in its darkness,
and the glory of all who serve your love.
I give you thanks, Beloved,
for ceaselessly you are giving us life,
bearing our pain, and making love with us,
this night and always.

Praying in Christ

Eternal Spirit,
Life-giver, Pain-bearer, Love-maker,
source of all that is and that shall be,
Father and Mother of us all,
loving God, in whom is heaven:

The hallowing of your name
echo through the universe.
The way of your justice
be followed by the peoples of the world.
Your heavenly will
be done by all created beings.
Your commonwealth of peace and freedom
sustain our hope and come on earth.

With the bread we need for today,
feed us.
In the hurts we absorb from one another,
forgive us.
In times of temptation and test,

strengthen us.
From trials too severe to endure,
spare us.
From the grip of all that is evil,
free us.

For you reign in the glory
of the power that is love,
now and for ever. Amen.

I will lie down in peace

I will lie down in peace and take my rest,
for it is in you alone that I dwell unafraid.
I embrace you, Life-giver, Pain-bearer, Love-maker,
I love you and adore you above all for ever.
May your name be revered beyond the furthest star,
delighted in and glorified above all for ever.

[Particular Prayers]

For peace

God of many names,
Lover of all peoples,
we pray for peace,
in our hearts,
in our homes,
in our nations,
in our world,
the peace of your will,
the peace of our need.

For refreshment

Be present, Spirit of God,
and renew us through the silent hours of this night,
so that we who are wearied
   by the changes and chances of this fleeting world,
may rest upon your eternal changelessness;
in the Spirit of Jesus Christ
our Guardian and our Guide.

Blessing

To God the Creator
who loved us first
and gave this world to be our home:

to God the Redeemer
who loves us and by dying and rising
pioneered the way of freedom:

to God the Sanctifier
who spreads the divine love in our hearts:

be praise and glory for time and for eternity.

The divine Spirit dwells in us:
Thanks be to God.

WEDNESDAY

Invocation

The angels of God guard us through the night,
and quieten the powers of darkness.
The Spirit of God be our guide
to lead us to peace and to glory.

Be alert;
stand firm in the faith;
be courageous and strong.
Let everything you do be done in love.

Our help is in the name of the eternal God,
who is making the heavens and the earth.

Thanksgiving

Dear God, thank you for all that is good,
for our creation and our humanity,
for the stewardship you have given us of this planet earth,
for the gifts of life and of one another,

for the people and events of this day . . .

for our ancestors, for the land, for this country . . .

for your love, unbounded and eternal . . .

O Thou, most holy and beloved,
my companion, my albatross, my guide upon the way.

Recognition

Hear the wisdom of Jesus:
Abide in my love.
Kyrie eleison.
Love your enemies.
Christe eleison.
Love your neighbour as yourself.
Kyrie eleison.
Love one another as I have loved you.
Christe eleison.
Above all, love God with the whole of your being.
Kyrie eleison . . .

God of forgiveness, we contemplate you.

You pour out your lifeblood in love for us,
you pursue us and disturb us and accept us,
you take to your heart our sin and pain,
the gift of a costly and infinite enduring,
you overcome evil with the goodness of love.

God of forgiveness, we contemplate you.

Psalms

Eternal Spirit, flow through our being and open our lips
that our mouths may proclaim your praise.
Let us worship the God of love:
Alleluia. Alleluia.

Always aware of us,
ever-present with us,
ceaselessly creating us –
we respond in love,
we tremble and adore,
our God, mysterious and faithful.

Light of light, you have searched me out and known me.
You know where I am and where I go,
you see my thoughts from afar.
You discern my paths and my resting places,
you are acquainted with all my ways.
Yes, and not a word comes from my lips
but you, O God, have heard it already.
You are in front of me and you are behind me,
you have laid your hand on my shoulder.
Such knowledge is too wonderful for me,
so great that I cannot fathom it.
Where shall I go from your Spirit,
where shall I flee from your presence?
If I climb to the heavens you are there:
if I descend to the depths of the earth you are there also.
If I spread my wings towards the morning,
and fly to the uttermost shores of the sea,
even there your hand will lead me,
and your right hand will hold me.

If I should cry to the darkness to cover me,
and the night to enclose me,
the darkness is no darkness to you,
and the night is as clear as the day.
For you have created every part of my being,
cell and tissue, blood and bone.
You have woven me in the womb of my mother;
I will praise you, so wonderfully am I made.
You know me to the very core of my being;
nothing in me was hidden from your eyes
when I was formed in silence and secrecy,
in intricate splendour in the depths of the earth.
Even as they were forming you saw my limbs,
each part of my body shaped by your finger.
How deep are your thoughts to me, O God,
how great is the sum of them.
Were I to count them they are more in number
than the grains of sand upon the sea-shore –
and still I would know nothing about you –
yet still would you hold me in the palm of your hand.

Always aware of us,
ever-present with us,
ceaselessly creating us –
we respond in love,
we tremble and adore,
our God, mysterious and faithful.

ReadingFirst

Wednesday of the month

There is no fear in love, but perfect love casts out fear.
For fear has to do with punishment,
and those who are afraid are not perfected in love.
We love because God first loved us.
If anyone says, I love God, and hates a brother or sister,
that person is a liar;
for those who do not love their brothers and sisters whom
　they have seen
cannot love God whom they have not seen.

Second Wednesday of the month

Living God, you are in the midst of us,
and we are called by your holy name:
leave us not, O God of Love.

Third Wednesday of the month

It is the God who said, Let light shine out of darkness,
who has shone in our hearts
to give the light of the knowledge of the glory of God
in the face of Jesus Christ.
But we have this treasure in earthen vessels,
to show that the transcendent power belongs to God and
　not to us.
We are afflicted in every way, but not crushed;
perplexed, but not driven to despair;
persecuted, but not forsaken;
struck down, but not destroyed;

always carrying about in us the death of Jesus,
so that the life of Jesus may also be manifested in our bodies.

Fourth Wednesday of the month

According to the riches of God's glory,
may we be strengthened with might
through the Holy Spirit in our inner being,
that being rooted and grounded in love,
we may have power to comprehend, with all the saints,
what is the breadth and length and height and depth,
and to know the love of God which surpasses knowledge,
that we may be filled with all the fullness of God.

29th, 30th and 31st of the month

Let justice flow on like a river,
and righteousness like an ever-flowing stream.

Hymn

Before the ending of the day,
Creator of the world, we pray
that you, with love and lasting light,
would guard us through the hours of night.

From all ill dreams defend our eyes,
from nightly fears and fantasies;
redeem through us our evil foe,
that we no lasting harm may know.

O wisest guide, grant all we ask,
fulfil in us your holy task,
surround us with your love and care,
and lead us on, your life to share.

All praise to God, sustaining us,
redeeming and transfiguring us,
thanksgiving in eternity,
all praise, beloved Trinity.

Into your hands

Living God, faithful and trustworthy,
delighting in me, yearning for me,
into your hands I cast the whole of my being,
for you are transforming me, bodily, spiritually.
Keep me, dear God, as the apple of your eye,
enfold me under the shadow of your wings.

Antiphon to the Nunc Dimittis

Inspire me while waking,
restore me while sleeping,
that awake in the night I may watch with Christ,
and asleep may rest in your peace.

An unfolding of the Nunc Dimittis

I give you thanks, Beloved,
I have lived to see this day.
Your promise is fulfilled,
and my duty done.

Each night you give me your peace,
for I have glimpsed with my own eyes
the liberation you prepare for all people,
a light to the world in its darkness,
and the glory of all who serve your love.
I give you thanks, Beloved,
for ceaselessly you are giving us life,
bearing our pain, and making love with us,
this night and always.

Praying in Christ

Abba, **our Father,**
Amma, **our Mother,**
Beloved, **our God,**
Creator of all:
your name be held holy,
your domain spread among us,
your wisdom be our guide,
your way be our path,
your will be done well,
at all times, in all places,
on earth as in heaven.
Give us the bread
we need for today,
the manna of your promise,
the taste of your tomorrow.
As we release those
indebted to us,
so forgive us our debts,
our trespass on others.
Fill us with courage
in time of our testing.

45

Spare us from trials
too severe to endure.
Free us from the grip
of the powers that bind.
For yours is the goodness
in which evil dissolves;
yours is the joy
that sounds through the pain;
yours is the life
which swallows up death.
Yours is the glory,
the transfiguring light,
the victory of love,
for time and eternity,
for age after age.
So be it. Amen.

I will lie down in peace

I will lie down in peace and take my rest,
for it is in you alone that I dwell unafraid.
I embrace you, Life-giver, Pain-bearer, Love-maker,
I love you and adore you above all for ever.
May your name be revered beyond the furthest star,
delighted in and glorified above all for ever.

[Particular Prayers]

For our work

Living God, whose glory shines through the heavens,
and whose handiwork the universe declares,

transform all our work and labour, our routines and
   craftsmanship,
emancipating them from the kingdom of mammon,
and making of them a work of ministry in your
   commonwealth of grace,
after the pattern of Jesus and in the power of the Spirit.

Greeting to our ancestors

The God of peace sanctify you completely,
even to the glory of the great day:
faithful is the God who calls,
the God whose promises will be fulfilled.

NN,
God bless you richly,
grow in grace,
make love,
keep us in loving mind,
hold us close in the Presence,
guide us,
pray for us.

Blessing

The grace of Jesus Christ,
the love of God,
and communion in the Holy Spirit,
be with us now and always.

The divine Spirit dwells in us:
thanks be to God.

THURSDAY

Invocation

The angels of God guard us through the night,
and quieten the powers of darkness.
The Spirit of God be our guide
to lead us to peace and to glory.

Pray in the power of the Spirit.
Keep watch and persevere,
and remember all God's people.

Our help is in the name of the eternal God,
who is making the heavens and the earth.

Thanksgiving

Dear God, thank you for all that is good,
for our creation and our humanity,
for the stewardship you have given us of this planet earth,
for the gifts of life and of one another,

for the people and events of this day . . .

for all the peoples and faiths of the world . . .

for your love, unbounded and eternal . . .

O Thou, most holy and beloved,
my companion, my pilgrim staff, my guide upon the way.

Recognition

Loving God, close your eyes to our sins,
we who have wounded your love.
Refine us with the flame of your Spirit:
cleanse us with springs of living water.
Save us with words of forgiveness and peace:
make us whole, steadfast in spirit.
Broken are our bones, yet you can heal us,
and we shall leap for joy and dance again . . .

God of love, we adore you.

You transfigure our disfigured faces,
you strive with our resistant clay,
you bring out of our chaos, harmony.

God of love, we adore you.

Psalms

Eternal Spirit, flow through our being and open our lips
that our mouths may proclaim your praise.
Let us worship the God of love:
Alleluia. Alleluia.

God is our refuge and strength,
a very present help in time of trouble.
Therefore we shall not be afraid,
even though the earth be moved,
even though the mountains should crumble and fall into
the sea,
even though the waters should foam and rage,
assault the cliffs and make them shudder.
You are for us the God of the powers,
a safe stronghold, the God of all peoples.

There is a river whose streams make glad the city of God.
Here is God's dwelling place and it will stand firm.
God's rescue dawns like the morning light,
God's voice echoes through every land.
When powerful nations panic and totter
and the whole world comes crashing down,
you are for us the God of the powers,
a safe stronghold, the God of all peoples.

Come and see, stand in awe
at the powerful things God will do on earth,
putting an end to all war in the world,
breaking the bow, shattering the spear into splinters,
throwing our weapons on the fire.
'Be still and know that I am God:
exalted among the nations,
my name known at last on the earth.'
You are for us the God of the powers,
a safe stronghold, the God of all peoples.

Silence

You are trustworthy and true, my God,
holding fast to your covenant of love.
You are trustworthy and true, my God,
holding fast to your covenant of love.

At nightfall I come to an inn on my journey,
a place of refuge, of your presence, O God,
a sanctuary, a temple, the tent of your dwelling,
where I lie down to sleep in safety.
Under the shade of your hovering wings
I have no fear of the unknown in the dark.
You have set me free from the snare of the hunter,
from the depth of the pit of snakes.
My trust in you keeps me from terror,
they sense no need to attack me.
You overshadow me with your wings,
I am safe under your feathers.
As a mother protects her brood,
so are you tender and strong towards me.
With your faithfulness as shield and defence,
I have courage to face any danger.
In the dead of night I have no terror to fear,
neither dread in the daytime the plunge of the dagger,
nor fear the plague that stalks in the darkness,
nor the fever that strikes in the heat of the day.
For you will command your angels
to keep me in your narrow ways:
they will bear me up in their hands
lest I dash my foot against a stone.
Because you are bound to me in love,
therefore you will deliver me.

You will lift me out of danger
because I hold on to your name.
You know me in intimate trust,
in my inner heart I am loyal and true
In my anguish and need you are with me,
you will set me free and clothe me with glory.
I shall live to be full of years,
I shall know the abundance of your salvation.

You are trustworthy and true, my God,
holding fast to your covenant of love.
You are trustworthy and true, my God,
holding fast to your covenant of love.

Reading

First Thursday of the month

Those who drink the water that I shall give them
    will never thirst:
it will become in them a bubbling spring,
welling up to eternal life.

Second Thursday of the month

God has not given us a spirit of fear,
but of power and of love and of a sound mind.

Third Thursday of the month

Abide in me and I in you:
as the branch cannot bear fruit of itself,
unless it abides in the vine,

neither can you
unless you abide in me.

Peace I leave with you,
my peace I give to you.
Let not your hearts be troubled,
neither let them be afraid.

Fourth Thursday of the month

The God who calls you is faithful.
The same God will enable you,
fulfilling the promise of old.

29th, 30th and 31st of the month

Do not urge me to go back and desert you.
Where you go, I shall go,
and where you stay, I shall stay.
Your people will be my people,
and your God shall be my God.
Where you die, I shall die,
and there be buried.
I solemnly declare before the Living One
that nothing but death will separate me from you.

Hymn

Be thou my vision, O Christ of my heart,
be all else but naught to me save that thou art,
be thou my best thought in the day and the night,
both waking and sleeping, thy presence my light.

Riches I heed not, nor vain empty praise,
be thou my inheritance now and always.
Be thou and thou only the first in my heart,
O Sovereign of heaven, my treasure thou art.

Into your hands

Living God, faithful and trustworthy,
delighting in me, yearning for me,
into your hands I cast the whole of my being,
for you are transforming me, bodily, spiritually.
Keep me, dear God, as the apple of your eye,
enfold me under the shadow of your wings.

Antiphon to the Nunc Dimittis

Inspire me while waking,
restore me while sleeping,
that awake in the night I may watch with Christ,
and asleep may rest in your peace.

An unfolding of the Nunc Dimittis

I give you thanks, Beloved,
I have lived to see this day.
Your promise is fulfilled,
and my duty done.

Each night you give me your peace,
for I have glimpsed with my own eyes
the liberation you prepare for all people,
a light to the world in its darkness,
and the glory of all who serve your love.
I give you thanks, Beloved,
for ceaselessly you are giving us life,
bearing our pain, and making love with us,
this night and always.

Praying in Christ

Eternal Spirit,
Life-giver, Pain-bearer, Love-maker,
source of all that is and that shall be,
Father and Mother of us all,
loving God, in whom is heaven:

The hallowing of your name
echo through the universe.
The way of your justice
be followed by the peoples of the world.
Your heavenly will
be done by all created beings.
Your commonwealth of peace and freedom
sustain our hope and come on earth.

With the bread we need for today,
feed us.
In the hurts we absorb from one another,
forgive us.
In times of temptation and test,
strengthen us.

From trials too severe to endure,
spare us.
From the grip of all that is evil,
free us.

For you reign in the glory
of the power that is love,
now and for ever. Amen.

I will lie down in peace

I will lie down in peace and take my rest,
for it is in you alone that I dwell unafraid.
I embrace you, Life-giver, Pain-bearer, Love-maker,
I love you and adore you above all for ever.
May your name be revered beyond the furthest star,
delighted in and glorified above all for ever.

[Particular Prayers]

For inner peace

Dear God,
from whom all holy desires,
all good counsels,
and all just works do proceed,
give unto thy servants that peace
which the world cannot give,
that our hearts may be set
to obey thy commandments,
and also that by thee,
we being defended from the fear of our enemies
may pass our time in rest and quietness;

through the universal Christ,
the maker of peace.

For the unity of humankind

We adore thee,
who art One
and who art Love;
and it is in unity and love
that we would live together,
doing thy will.

Blessing

The blessing of God,
giver of life,
bearer of pain,
maker of love,
be with us now and always.

The divine Spirit dwells in us:
Thanks be to God.

FRIDAY

Invocation

The angels of God guard us through the night,
and quieten the powers of darkness.
The Spirit of God be our guide
to lead us to peace and to glory.

Jesus said to his disciples,
Were you not able to stay awake for one hour?
Keep watch, all of you,
and pray that you will not fail in time of testing.

Our help is in the name of the eternal God,
who is making the heavens and the earth.

Thanksgiving

Dear God, thank you for all that is good,
for our creation and our humanity,
for the stewardship you have given us of this planet earth,
for the gifts of life and of one another,

for the people and events of this day . . .

for friends and families . . .

for all that you have given us through Jesus of Nazareth . . .

O Thou, most holy and beloved,
my companion, my desert bread, my guide upon the way.

Recognition

We confess our unfaithfulness:
our pride, hypocrisy and impatience;
our self-indulgent appetites and ways;
our exploitation of other people;
the violence, envy and ruthless greed
in our hearts and deeds;
our idleness in ease and comfort,
and our possessiveness;
our neglect of prayer,
and our failure to live our faith . . .

God of holiness, we tremble in your presence.

You show us how far we have wandered in a land that is
     waste,
you face us with the truth of our lack of love,
you uncover the layers of our delusions,
you pierce us with the laser that heals,
you embrace us with a refining fire,
you refuse to let us go.

God of holiness, we tremble in your presence.

Psalms

Eternal Spirit, flow through our being and open our lips
that our mouths may proclaim your praise.
Let us worship the God of love:
Alleluia. Alleluia.

Costing not less than everything,
all manner of things shall be well.
Costing not less than everything,
all manner of things shall be well.

Empty, exhausted, and ravaged,
in the depths of despair I writhe.
Anguished and afflicted, terribly alone,
I trudge a bleak wasteland, devoid of all love.
In the echoing abyss I call out:
no God of compassion hears my voice.
Yet still I pray, Open your heart,
for my tears well up within me.
If you keep account of all that drags me down,
there is no way I can stand firm.
Paralysed and powerless, I topple over,
bound by the evil I hate.
But with you is forgiveness and grace,
there is nothing I can give – it seems like a death.
The power of your love is so awesome:
I am terrified by your freeing embrace.
Drawn from the murky depths by a fish hook,
I shout to the air that will kill me:
Must I leave behind all that I cherish
before I can truly breathe free?

Suspended between one world and the next,
I waited for you, my God.
Apprehension and hope struggled within me,
I waited, I longed for your word.
As a watchman waits for the morning,
through the darkest and coldest of nights,
more even than the watchman who peers through the gloom,
I hope for the dawn, I yearn for the light.
You will fulfil your promise to bring me alive,
overflowing with generous love.
You will free me from the grip of evil,
O God of mercy and compassion.
Touching and healing the whole of my being,
you are a God whose reach has no limit.
All that has been lost will one day be found:
the communion of the rescued will rejoice in your name.

Costing not less than everything,
all manner of things shall be well.
Costing not less than everything,
all manner of things shall be well.

Silence

Home at last, contented and grateful.
Home at last, contented and grateful.

When God takes us home from our exile,
we shall wake from this nightmare and live again.
Bars of iron will be shattered: we shall walk free
from gulag and ghetto, from dungeon and tower.
We shall sing and laugh for joy,
echoed by birdsong and breeze of the spring.

The land itself will rejoice in God,
the whole world give praise for the wonders we have seen.
Lead us home, renew our hope, bring us to life,
like impossible rivers in the cursed and barren desert.
We go on our way sadly, with tears sowing seeds that will die,
we shall return with joy, with gladness bearing our sheaves.

Home at last, contented and grateful.
Home at last, contented and grateful.

Reading

First Friday of the month

This is my commandment,
that you love one another,
even as I have loved you.
You can have no greater love than this,
than to lay down your life for your friends.
You are my friends, if you do what I command you.
No longer do I call you servants,
for a servant does not know what his master is doing.
I have called you friends,
because I have disclosed to you
everything that I heard from my Father.

Second Friday of the month

All you who are led by the Spirit of God are children of
    God . . .

For you did not receive the spirit of fear,
but you have received the spirit of adoption . . .

When we cry, Abba, Father,
it is the Spirit bearing witness with our spirit
that we are children of God . . .

and if children, then heirs,
heirs of God and fellow-heirs with Christ . . .

provided we suffer with him
that we may also be glorified with him.

Third Friday of the month

We know that the whole creation itself
will be set free from its bondage to decay,
having been groaning in travail together until now;
and not only the creation, but we ourselves,
who have the first fruits of the Spirit,
groan inwardly as we wait for our adoption as sons and
    daughters,
the redemption of our bodies,
and obtain the glorious liberty of the children of God.

Fourth Friday of the month

I am sure there is nothing in life or in death,
no powers that be, no evil's grip,
in the world as it is or the world as it shall be,
nothing in the whole of creation
that can separate us from the love of God in Christ Jesus.

29th, 30th and 31st of the month

You desire our steadfast love,
not the rituals and habits we build out of fear.
You yearn for us to offer our hearts and our lives,
that we might act justly, love kindness,
and walk humbly with you, our God.

Hymn

O thou who camest from above
the fire celestial to impart,
kindle a flame of sacred love
on the low altar of my heart.

There let it for thy glory burn
with inextinguishable blaze,
and trembling to its source return
in humble prayer and fervent praise.

Jesus confirm my heart's desire
to work and speak and think for thee,
still let me guard the holy fire,
and still stir up thy gift in me.

Ready for all thy perfect will,
my acts of faith and love repeat,
till death thine endless mercies seal,
and make the sacrifice complete.

Into your hands

Living God, faithful and trustworthy,
delighting in me, yearning for me,
into your hands I cast the whole of my being,
for you are transforming me, bodily, spiritually.
Keep me, dear God, as the apple of your eye,
enfold me under the shadow of your wings.

Antiphon to the Nunc Dimittis

Inspire me while waking,
restore me while sleeping,
that awake in the night I may watch with Christ,
and asleep may rest in your peace.

An unfolding of the Nunc Dimittis

I give you thanks, Beloved,
I have lived to see this day.
Your promise is fulfilled,
and my duty done.
Each night you give me your peace,
for I have glimpsed with my own eyes
the liberation you prepare for all people,
a light to the world in its darkness,
and the glory of all who serve your love.
I give you thanks, Beloved,
for ceaselessly you are giving us life,
bearing our pain, and making love with us,
this night and always.

Praying in Christ

Dear God, our Creator,
beloved companion and guide upon the way,
eternal Spirit within us and beyond us.
Let us honour your name
in lives of costly, giving love.
Let us show that we and all whom we meet
deserve dignity and respect,
for they are your dwelling place and your home.
Let us share in action
your deep desire for justice and peace
among the peoples of the world.
Let us share our bread with one another,
the bread that you have shared with us.
Let us in the spirit of your forgiving us,
make friends with those we have harmed
    and failed to love.
Let us overcome our trials and temptations,
our suffering and dying,
in the strength and courage
with which you overcame them too.
Let us in your love free the world from evil,
transforming darkness into light.
For the whole universe is yours,
and you invite us to be partners
in the work of your creating.
Amen.
So be it. So will we do it.

I will lie down in peace

I will lie down in peace and take my rest,
for it is in you alone that I dwell unafraid.
I embrace you, Life-giver, Pain-bearer, Love-maker,
I love you and adore you above all for ever.
May your name be revered beyond the furthest star,
delighted in and glorified above all for ever.

[Particular Prayers]

Christ crucified

Christ crucified, nailed to the unyielding wood,
bearer to us of the true and living God,
give us courage to face what must decay,
the disintegration of our mortal flesh,
and give us faith to shed our false and deadly selves,
to let them be as smoke vanishing in the evening breeze,
that as soul-bodies we may grow through all our days
refined to a finer tuning than we can yet discern,
shaped into the likeness of your transfigured, risen body,
that our true and lively selves, fresh embodied,
living flames at last,
may dwell and dance with you, in love, for ever.

Lighten our darkness

Lighten our darkness, we ask of you, dear God,
and in your great mercy strengthen us
to face the perils and dangers of the night;
for the love of your well-beloved Son,
our Liberator and our Healer, Jesus Christ.

Blessing

The blessing of God,
the shalom of God,
the wildness and the warmth of God,
be among us and between us,
now and always.

The divine Spirit dwells in us:
Thanks be to God.

SATURDAY

Invocation

The angels of God guard us through the night,
and quieten the powers of darkness.
The Spirit of God be our guide
to lead us to peace and to glory.

It is but lost labour that you haste to rise up early,
and so late take rest,
and eat the bread of anxiety.
For those beloved of God are given gifts even while they
  sleep.

Our help is in the name of the eternal God,
who is making the heavens and the earth.

Thanksgiving

Dear God, thank you for all that is good,
for our creation and our humanity,
for the stewardship you have given us of this planet earth,
for the gifts of life and of one another,

for the people and events of this day . . .

for the communion of saints . . .

for your love, unbounded and eternal . . .

O Thou, most holy and beloved,
my companion, my counsellor, my guide upon the way.

Recognition

We repent the wrongs we have done:
our blindness to human need and suffering;
our indifference to injustice and cruelty;
our false judgements, petty thoughts, and contempt;
our waste and pollution of the earth and oceans;
our lack of concern for those who come after us;
our complicity in the making of instruments of mass
  destruction,
and our threatening their use . . .

Eternal Spirit, living God,
in whom we live and move and have our being,
all that we are, have been, and shall be is known to you,
to the secrets of our hearts, and all that rises to trouble us.
Living flame, burn into us;
cleansing wind, scour through us;
fountain of water, well up within us,
that we may love and praise in deed and in truth.

Psalms

Eternal Spirit, flow through our being and open our lips
that our mouths may proclaim your praise.
Let us worship the God of love:
Alleluia. Alleluia.

As a deer longs for streams of water,
so longs my soul for you, O God.
My soul is thirsty for the living God:
when shall I draw near to see your face?
My tears have been my food in the night:
all day long they ask me, Where now is your God?
As I pour out my soul in distress,
I remember how I went to the temple of God,
with shouts and songs of thanksgiving,
a multitude keeping high festival.

Why are you so full of heaviness, my soul,
and why so rebellious within me?
Put your trust in God, patiently wait for the dawn:
you will then praise your deliverer and your God.

Pause

My soul is heavy within me: therefore I remember you
from the land of Jordan and from the hills of Hermon.
Deep calls to deep in the roar of the waterfalls,
all your waves and your torrents have gone over me.
Surely, O God, you will show me mercy in the daytime,
and at night I will sing your praise, O God my God.
I will say to God, my rock, Why have you forgotten me?

Why must I go like a mourner because the enemy oppresses
   me?
Like a sword piercing my bones, my enemies have mocked
   me,
asking me all day long, Where now is your God?

Why are you so full of heaviness, my soul,
and why so rebellious within me?
Put your trust in God, patiently wait for the dawn:
you will then praise your deliverer and your God.

Pause

O God, take up my cause and strive for me
with a godless people that knows no mercy.
Save me from the grip of cunning and lies,
for you are my God and my strength.
Why must you cast me away from your presence?
Why must I be clothed in rags, humiliated by my enemy?
O send out your light and your truth and let them lead me,
let them guide me to your holy hill and to your dwelling.
Then I shall go to the altar of God, the God of my joy and
   delight,
and to the harp I shall sing your praises, O God my God.

Why are you so full of heaviness, my soul,
and why so rebellious within me?
Put your trust in God, patiently wait for the dawn:
you will then praise your deliverer and your God.

Reading

First Saturday of the month

There is great gain in godliness with contentment.
For we brought nothing into this world,
and we cannot take anything out of it.
But if we have food and clothing,
with these we shall be content . . .

For the love of money is the root of all evils . . .

So shun all this:
aim at justice, Christlikeness,
fidelity, steadfastness, gentleness . . .

Second Saturday of the month

Open your mouth for the dumb,
for the rights of those who are left desolate.
Open your mouth, judge righteously,
maintain the rights of the poor and the needy.

Third Saturday of the month

Though our outer nature is wasting away,
our inner nature is being renewed every day.
For this slight momentary affliction
is preparing for us an eternal weight of glory beyond
    comparison,
because we look not to the things that are seen,
but to the things that are unseen;

73

for the things that are seen are transient,
but the things that are unseen are eternal.

Fourth Saturday of the month

The Spirit of God is upon me,
anointing me to preach good news to the poor,
sending me to proclaim release to the captives
and recovery of sight to the blind,
to set at liberty those who are oppressed,
to proclaim the time of God's grace and favour.

29th, 30th and 31st of the month

Thus says the Living One:
I shall lead you into the desert,
I shall lure you into the wilderness.
And I shall speak to your heart there,
with words of great tenderness.

Hymn

**Be still in God's presence,
be still in God's presence,
be still in God's presence,
and love and be loved.**

**Be still in God's presence,
be still in God's presence,
be still in God's presence,
and love and be loved.**

Fall deep in the silence,
fall deep in the silence,
fall deep in the silence,
  the silence of God.

Fall deep in the silence,
fall deep in the silence,
fall deep in the silence,
  the silence of God.

Into your hands

Living God, faithful and trustworthy,
delighting in me, yearning for me,
into your hands I cast the whole of my being,
for you are transforming me, bodily, spiritually.
Keep me, dear God, as the apple of your eye,
enfold me under the shadow of your wings.

Antiphon to the Nunc Dimittis

Inspire me while waking,
restore me while sleeping,
that awake in the night I may watch with Christ,
and asleep may rest in your peace.

An unfolding of the Nunc Dimittis

I give you thanks, Beloved,
I have lived to see this day.

Your promise is fulfilled,
and my duty done.
Each night you give me your peace,
for I have glimpsed with my own eyes
the liberation you prepare for all people,
a light to the world in its darkness,
and the glory of all who serve your love.
I give you thanks, Beloved,
for ceaselessly you are giving us life,
bearing our pain, and making love with us,
this night and always.

Praying in Christ

Abba, **our Father,**
Amma, **our Mother,**
Beloved, **our God,**
Creator of all:
your name be held holy,
your domain spread among us,
your wisdom be our guide,
your way be our path,
your will be done well,
at all times, in all places,
on earth as in heaven.
Give us the bread
we need for today,
the manna of your promise,
the taste of your tomorrow.
As we release those
indebted to us,

so forgive us our debts,
our trespass on others.
Fill us with courage
in time of our testing.
Spare us from trials
too severe to endure.
Free us from the grip
of the powers that bind.
For yours is the goodness
in which evil dissolves;
yours is the joy
that sounds through the pain;
yours is the life
which swallows up death.
Yours is the glory,
the transfiguring light,
the victory of love,
for time and eternity,
for age after age.
So be it. Amen.

I will lie down in peace

I will lie down in peace and take my rest,
for it is in you alone that I dwell unafraid.
I embrace you, Life-giver, Pain-bearer, Love-maker,
I love you and adore you above all for ever.
May your name be revered beyond the furthest star,
delighted in and glorified above all for ever.

[Particular Prayers]

Loving God

Loving God,
you have prepared for those who love you
such good things as pass our understanding
pour into our hearts such love towards you,
that we may love you in all things,
and love you beyond everything,
and so inherit your promises,
which exceed all we can desire,
in Jesus Christ, ever-loving and ever-beloved.

Abiding and increasing

Indwelling God,
strengthen your servants with your heavenly grace,
that we may continue yours for ever,
and daily increase in your Holy Spirit more and more
until we come to share in the glory of your Kingdom.

Blessing

Blessing, light and glory surround us
and scatter the darkness of the long and lonely night.

The divine Spirit dwells in us:
Thanks be to God.

READINGS
AND
ANTIPHONS TO THE
NUNC DIMITTIS
for special days and seasons

ADVENT

Reading

A voice cries,
In the wilderness prepare the way of the Living One;
make straight in the desert a highway for our God.
Every valley shall be lifted up,
and every mountain and hill made low:
the uneven ground shall become level,
and the rough places a plain.
And the glory of God shall be revealed,
and all flesh shall see it together.

Antiphon

Come, O God, and visit us in peace,
that we may rejoice in your presence with a perfect heart.

CHRISTMAS

Reading

The Word became flesh and dwelt among us.
We beheld the glory of God shining through a human face,
as a mother's eyes live through her daughter's,
and as a son reflects his father's image,
the glory of God in a human being fully alive.

Antiphon

Alleluia. The Word was made flesh. Alleluia.
And dwelt among us, Alleluia, Alleluia.

EPIPHANY

Reading

Our eyes have seen your salvation,
which you have prepared for all people,
a light to enlighten the nations,
and give glory to your people Israel.

Antiphon

Alleluia. All nations shall come before God. Alleluia.
And they will glorify God's holy name. Alleluia. Alleluia.

LENT

Reading

Is not this the fast that I choose:
to loose the bonds of wickedness,
to undo the thong of the yoke,
to let the oppressed go free,
and to break every prison bar?
Is it not to share your bread with the hungry,
and to bring the homeless poor into your house,
when you see the naked, to cover him,
and not to hide yourself from your own flesh?
Then shall your light break forth as the dawn,
and your healing shall spring up speedily.

Antiphon

For their sake I consecrate myself,
that they also may be consecrated in truth.

PASSIONTIDE

Reading

Come, let us turn again to the living God,
the God whose love sears and refines us.
For you have torn us and you will heal us,
you have stricken us and you will bind us up.
After two days you will revive us:
on the third day you will raise us up.

Antiphon

Christ became obedient to death,
even death on a cross.

EASTER

Reading

Christ is risen from the dead,
and become the first fruits of those who slept.
As death came into the world by a human being,
so also has come the resurrection from the dead.
For as in Adam all die,
even so in Christ shall all be made alive.

Antiphon

Alleluia. Christ is risen. Alleluia.
He is risen indeed. Alleluia, Alleluia.

ASCENSION

Reading

Christ reigns, disarming the overweening powers,
dissolving evil, transfiguring pain, swallowing death.
Christ is with us always, to the end of time.

Antiphon

Alleluia. The pioneer of our salvation has triumphed
    over suffering and death. Alleluia.
The firstborn among many sisters and brothers
    has led the way into the presence of God.
    Alleluia. Alleluia.

PENTECOST

Reading

The love of God has been shed abroad in our hearts
through the Holy Spirit who has been given to us.
For God has not given us a spirit of fear,
but of power and of love and of a sound mind.

Antiphon

Alleluia. The Holy Spirit will teach you all things. Alleluia.
And will guide you into all truth. Alleluia. Alleluia.

TRINITY

Reading

Countless angels praise you
and sing to you with ceaseless voice:
Holy, holy, holy is God,
who was and who is and who is to come. Amen.
Blessing and glory and wisdom and thanksgiving
and power and love be to our God for ever and ever.

Antiphon

Alleluia. Great praise and everlasting glory be to God,
  Lover, Beloved, Mutual Friend. Alleluia.
Life-giver, Pain-bearer, Love-maker. Alleluia. Alleluia.

SAINTS' DAYS

Reading

These are the words of the First and the Last,
who was dead and came to life again.
To those who are victorious
I shall give the right to eat from the tree of life
that stands in the Garden of God, alleluia.
Be faithful to death,
and I shall give you the crown of life. Alleluia.
To those who are victorious
I shall give some of the hidden manna.
I shall them also a white stone, alleluia.
And on the stone will be written a new name,
known only to the one who receives it, alleluia.

Antiphon

Alleluia. The Lamb who was slain has conquered. Alleluia.
All who follow the Way will share in the victory.
Alleluia. Alleluia.

THE DEPARTED

Reading

Thanks be to God
because in Christ's victory over the grave
a new age has dawned,
the reign of sin is over,
a broken world is being renewed,
and we are once again made whole.
As we believe that Jesus died and rose again,
so we believe it will be for those who have died:
God will bring them to life with Christ Jesus.

Antiphon

Give rest, O Christ,
to your servant(s) with your saints,
where sorrow and pain are no more,
neither sighing, but life everlasting.

PARTICULAR PRAYERS

Some blank pages follow for you to add prayers
for people and concerns close to your own heart

SUNDAY

MONDAY

TUESDAY

WEDNESDAY

THURSDAY

FRIDAY

SATURDAY

ADDITIONAL PRAYERS

IN THE LIFE OF THE CITY
AT NIGHT

the Spirit is suffering, striving, creating . . .

Blessings, guidance, and fierce and tender love
for those who are awake while others sleep:

on night shifts in factories . . .

watching over buildings . . .

travelling through the city . . .

cleaning offices . . .

stocking supermarket shelves . . .

in ambulances, fire engines, police cars . . .

observing and researching . . .

alert at power stations and waterworks . . .

at telephone exchanges . . .

at parties and night clubs . . .

driving taxis, buses, coaches, trams, trains . . .

flying over the city in planes . . .

speeding by the city on motorways . . .

thieving and attacking in the dark . . .

searching out the secrets of others . . .

hustling and walking the streets . . .

huddling in doorways . . .

listening to those in despair . . .

crying out in loneliness . . .

suddenly taken ill . . .

trying to sleep but cannot . . .

restless and awake in hospital . . .

coping with crises . . .

watching and caring . . .

giving birth . . .

awake with young children . . .

calming the confused . . .

praying through the darkness . . .

dying at home, in hospice or hospital . . .

keeping vigil with them . . .

. . . and those on the other side of the world

for whom it is day . . .

GOD BE . . .

God be in my head and in my understanding . . .
God be in my eyes and in my looking . . .
God be in my mouth and in my speaking . . .
God be in my tongue and in my tasting . . .
God be in my lips and in my greeting . . .

God be in my nose and in my scenting . . .
God be in my ears and in my hearing . . .
God be in my neck and in my humbling . . .
God be in my shoulders and in my bearing . . .
God be in my back and in my standing . . .

God be in my arms and in my reaching . . .
God be in my hands and in my working . . .
God be in my legs and in my walking . . .
God be in my feet and in my grounding . . .
God be in my joints and in my relating . . .

God be in my guts and in my feeling . . .
God be in my bowels and in my forgiving . . .
God be in my loins and in my swiving . . .
God be in my lungs and in my breathing . . .
God be in my heart and in my loving . . .

God be in my skin and in my touching . . .
God be in my flesh and in my yearning . . .
God be in my blood and in my living . . .
God be in my bones and in my dying . . .
God be at my end and at my beginning . . .

TO THE TROUBLING UNKNOWN

To the powers of dis-ease within us
and among us and through the world,
troubling us, entangling us, distracting us,
wounding us, holding us in their grip . . .

whatever be your name,
greed, pride, malice, envy, evil,
grief, rage, fear, pain, death . . .

known in the secret places of our hearts,
or as yet unknown to us,
or greater in strength than any one of us can bear alone,
come out of the darkness into light,
into the Presence, the Mystery, the Power,
of the pain-bearing, love-making, life-giving One . . .

that we may understand and withstand you,
that we may know your name and nature,
that you may ease your grip upon us,
that you may wound us no more . . .

that you may be transformed by the power
of that love that is deeper than the deepest pain,
so yielding your energy in the service of God,
freeing us together to be the friends of God,
and to live to reflect God's glory . . .

And where, through lack of prayer or fasting,
through weak will or faint heart,
through the mysteries of the unresolved,
through fear of your power to destroy,
we cannot yet be reconciled,
leave us be, and trouble us not tonight,
and wait awhile constrained,
until together we can face the refining, warming,
life-enhancing flame of the judging, healing, loving
    God . . .

THE FAUNA OF THE NIGHT

The fauna of the night,
hidden in the grass of your neglect . . .

Encounter them . . .
Contemplate them . . .
Dare to look steadily at them . . .
Wrestle with them . . .
Expect to be wounded in the struggle with them . . .
Name them . . .
Recognize them . . .
And be blessed by them . . .

At the breaking of dawn
they will be known as wonderful, life-giving creatures,
no longer exiled but returned to you,
made precious again,
moving with you into the future,
robed as destinies.

DARK ANGELS

You are troubled by your dark angels . . .

You seek to tame their wildness . . .

But they are the source of creativity within you . . .

If you deny them, banish them, seek to destroy them,
they will drain you of passion as they retreat,
and you will become pale and lifeless . . .

And if they should return and storm your gates,
you would be sore wounded . . .

However dark,
they are still angels,
guardians and protectors too . . .

THE WARMING OF FEAR

A prayer in twelve breaths

As you breathe in slowly and gently, say these words silently:
Breathing in love . . .

and as you breathe out slowly and gently, say these lines, one on each out breath:

The ice of my fear drips . . .

My crust self crumbles . . .

My fearful self melts . . .

My surface self yields . . .

I am yours, all is yours . . .

Little One, Great One . . .

I live in you, you live in me . . .

My smoke self vanishes . . .

My flame self glows . . .

Wholeheartedly I yearn . . .

heart-warming, heart-hatching . . .

I am strangely at home . . .

A PRAYER OF SURRENDER

Abba, Amma, Beloved, I abandon myself into your hands . . .
In your love for me, do as you will . . .
Whatever that may prove to be, I am thankful . . .
I am ready for all, I accept all . . .
Let only your will be done in me, as in all your creatures,
and I will ask nothing else . . .
Into your hands I commend the whole of my being . . .
I give you myself with the love of my heart . . .
For I love you, my God, and so I need to give . . .
to surrender myself into your hands . . .
with a trust beyond measure . . .
For you are my faithful Creator . . .
Abba . . . Amma . . .
Beloved . . .
Friend . . .

GOD'S COVENANT WITH ME/US

I Who Am and Who Shall Be,
Love-making Spirit within you,
Pain-bearing Presence beside you,
Life-giving Future before you,
I call you into being and bind myself to you.
By my own name and nature, in every eternal moment,
I affirm and renew my covenant,
I fulfil my deepest promise,
to love you to glory for ever,
to honour you as my home,
and to be loyal to you,
and full of faith in you,
our life-day long.
Amen. So be it.

MY/OUR COVENANT WITH GOD

Beloved and faithful Creator,
Love-making Spirit within me,
Pain-bearing Presence beside me,
Life-giving Future before me,
of my own free will I choose to share my life with you.
This and all my days
I affirm and renew my covenant,
I fulfil my deepest promise,
to love you in friendship for ever,
to honour you as my home,
and to be loyal to you,
and full of faith in you,
our life-day long.
Amen. So be it.

A COVENANT OF FRIENDSHIP

In the wonderful Mystery of God,
Love-making Spirit between us,
Pain-bearing Presence beside us,
Life-giving Future before us,
you have been given to me,
to be cherished in friendship.
By my own free will and destiny
I choose to share my life with you.
With and in that greater Love
I promise to do all that I can for your well-being for ever,
to honour you as Gods' home,
and to be loyal to you,
and full of faith in you,
our life-day long.
Amen. So be it.

FOR FRIENDS, HERE AND BEYOND

God of the living,
in whose embrace all creatures live,
in whatever world or condition they may be,
I remember in prayer those
whose names and needs and dwelling place
are known to you,
giving you thanks for them,
and for my memories of them.
In you, dear God, I love them.
May these waves of prayerful love
minister to their peace
and to their growth in love . . .
I pray in and through Jesus Christ,
who broke the barrier
of time and space and death
and is alive for ever.

WAYMARKS

THOUGHTS FOR THE NIGHT

JANUARY

1

A hooded stranger on horseback emerges from the mist. Do I expect an enemy, or at least bad news? Or a long-lost friend recognized in a moment of wonder, even in the darkness?

2

It may be the 'strange meeting' (of Wilfrid Owen's poem) between two soldiers, with the hard dark work to be done after the moment of recognition, 'I am the enemy you killed, my friend.'

3

I am invited to pray with open hand, not with clenched fist, though I may have to begin the journey into the dark by shaking my fist at the strange and fearful God of the night.

4

The surrender of myself in trust may be crucial at some point on the journey, but not at the beginning. Betrayals in the secret darkness of the past are not lightly undone.

5

Dig through unrelenting rock into matter that appears to be death-dealing. It is only deep below the surface that diamonds wait to be unearthed. Riddle the gravel in patient search for rare gold.

6

There is hard labour, a seeming waste of time and effort, a grinding small of surface self. Even if hope is alive, it is sparse. Even if there is a vein of mercy in the hard stone, it is thin.

7

Let eye and ear be keenly attentive to everything that is there, hidden deep within you in the dark. Only in time, and then when least expected, will you hear, welling up within you, your own true voice.

8

To embark on an exploration of our Everests and Antarcticas, storm-bound and through long nights, any contemplation of your underground caves, far from the sun, is daunting and demanding.

9

To set out on an adventure is 'to come against' whatever you may meet, *ad-venire* in Latin. You will find that you are up against it – howling wind, deafening silence, lost, with no sense of direction.

10

Keep moving, however slowly, through the dark caverns, simply recognizing your hatred of yourself, internalized from stigma and misuse of power, your lack of self-worth, your desire for control.

11

Slow down and simply be in the darkness. Keep breathing. Keep looking. Keep listening. Be steady. Be courageous. The light *will* pierce. The way *will* open up. You *will* emerge more whole.

12

Look for the hidden things, the creatures of your dreams, the storehouse of forgotten memories and hurts. Down at the source of your being may you recognize who you are and hear your true name. *[After George Appleton]*

13

Wrestle with the Stranger of the night, wrestle until the break of day, with the one who wounds you in thigh and groin, drawing from you with great reluctance the truth of your nature and your name.

14

In the struggle with the Stranger, as you recognize the deepest truths, be blessed as you limp into the dawn, ready for the embrace of the one who has forgiven you, the one you have refused for so long.

15

The frontiers of the familiar are closed to you: gardens and houses are but oases on the journey, which you need and which you need to love, but they are never the place of your struggle and creativity.

16

You have to be a pioneer, journeying to places which the rest of the world ignores – the Somme, Auschwitz, Hiroshima – humbly opening yourself to what others do not wish to see, both good and evil.

17

Such places *are* a wilderness: but take them to your heart and bless them. For the Lover lures you into the desert, where you will hear a voice deep in your being, far into the silence of the night.

18

It *is* a narrow way: but do not complain – the Way chose you, and you must be thankful. It *is* a difficult choice: but to choose what is difficult as if it were easy, *that* is faith. *[After W. H. Auden]*

19

Do not retreat from the unfamiliar out of fear, nor condemn it because it bewilders you. When a civilization turns, God may not be found at the old landmarks.

20

Listen to the outcast within you, the only one who can redeem you at the auction of your slavery, the only one who
can whisper the saving truth to your crumbling strength.

21

Listen to the outcast within you, who, scapegoated and
stigmatized, discovers the spring in the desert, holds water
to your parched lips, and embraces you with warmth, melting your frozen heart.

22

Listen to the outcast within you, who, silenced through
long fear of you, has learned a wisdom that you desper-
ately need, whom you can trust to befriend you, strangers
though you have become.

23

Listen not to the fury but to the zephyrs; not to the clamour, but to the whispers; not to the confusion, but to the
heartbeat; not to the chatter, but to the silence; not to the
surface discord, but to the deep harmony.

24

Listen to the inscape of your neglected soul, where the
voices of the poor and oppressed bring unimagined gifts
to your tyrant surface self – just as in the landscape of the
outer world.

25

Listen to what you have neglected, to what has grown monstrous because unrecognized. Fierce dragons guard rare treasure: dare to face them and they will become your allies.

26

Those 'others' of whom you are afraid, they too are your allies and can become your friends. Have compassion on them, create a place of welcome in your heart and in your home.

27

The usual and the frequent may be the statistical norm: they are not necessarily normal. Who are the ones your malign eye rejects, and who are the ones your benign eye especially favours? And God's eye?

28

Be patient towards the unresolved: love the questions themselves, and live them now. Gradually, without realizing it, in the distant future, you may come to live into the answers. *[After R. M. Rilke]*

29

When the desire rises to seize or grab, and you act immediately, you are trying to escape into comfort or excitement from the discomfort that grows if you have to wait, the hunger, the loneliness.

30

It takes courage to pause, to be still, to be patient, to *go through* the distressing feelings without of necessity acting them out. Recognize them, speak to them, and they will lose their grip on you.

31

Lay aside your habitual self-hatred, your refusal to accept your own worth and dignity. Love yourself. You cannot make yourself special; you simply *are* special. But it takes courage to receive this truth.

FEBRUARY

1

Taste what comes to you if you will, but pause, and only then decide whether to swallow or spit. Only so do you learn not to react but to respond – from inner truth not from surface delusion.

2

Now you can ask for what you need, not taking refusal for rejection, expectant of being surprised by unpredictable gifts, *knowing* the difference between compulsive searching and shared connecting.

3

The times of waiting expectantly are part of the journey into 'God', but there will be moments, hidden or spectacular, when you become aware of the Mystery of the Other Within.

4

In encountering the Mystery, the Universal Loving, engaging with your half-hearted loving, you discover that you have been 're-placed' in truth and that you can move towards the stranger without fear.

5

To be alone is simply to be at a distance, in bathroom or crowded cafe. To be lonely is to dislike being alone, becoming cramped and embittered. Here is another power to face with courage.

6

To embrace solitude is to be in touch with the springs of your own creativity. It is to be aware that you can never be separate from anyone. It is to know deep down what it is to love and be loved.

7

For Rilke, human beings are struggling to shape their loving anew, that of two solitudes who protect and border (or touch) and salute (or greet) each other.

8

For Laurens van der Post, when a whole civilization goes through a dark night, only those who can accept the journey through the dark side of being alone can be true companions to each other.

9

You cannot avoid being wounded, but you may find courage to grow through your suffering, refusing to sink into bitterness, transforming grief to compassion, producing fruit strange and unexpected.

10

For R. S. Shannon, the wounded oyster changes grit to pearl; for Léon Bloy, our hearts are wounded, even broken, that something new may come to life in us.

11

For a character in one of Charles Williams' novels, the challenge is to live from the depths of our wounds, to make the extent of our desolation the extent of our realm.

12

Your intrinsic tenderness may have been violated in early days beyond recall, and you seize up, afraid of intimacy. Seek your own hurt child, who waits and longs to speak to you in the language of those wounds. *[After W. H. Auden]*

13

Your inner child needs your adult caring strength in order to begin to trust again, so that the gifts may be released that have for so long been hidden away.

14

For John Collis, tensions remained from being a rejected twin, but he used the taut strings to make music that otherwise would not have been heard. Could he have denied such a calling for the sake of ease?

15

There is a pain, a wound, a sorrow, that cannot be taken away. It can only be endured, lived through, and in the process sometimes (though not always) transformed – the once in a while parable of hope.

16

As a wounded body who can you trust to touch you without harm, with hands that hold but do not intrude? Can you summon up the courage to ask for the touch that makes you feel accepted and loved?

17

In the solidarity of pain you can begin to mould it, to use this very raw material to shape – what? There are no words for it. Is it a 'glory' that has not yet been born?

18

In the bearing together of our pain, not fighting it or increasing it, we may discover a light that penetrates the dark places and a wisdom that uses the power of the dark to create what is new in the world.

19

If you have been somewhat healed of great harm, you can give hope to others only if the scars are visible, only if the suffering has been transformed to the deep compassion of an aching loving heart.

20

For Milosz, prayer is the source of life, but it is the prayer that comes not from the mouth but 'from the lips of wounds'.

21

For Angelus Silesius,
   There is no higher aim than to reclaim another, blinded by life's pain, to help him see and live again.

22

You lie awake, aware of your body. Love your body. You *are* a body: not a no-body, not just any-body, but some-body. And *we* are a Body, a Living Organism, for some the 'Body of Christ'.

23

God is at the heart of your striving, of your giving and receiving, drawing you closer in the energies of loving, always pursuing, luring, inviting, never letting go.

24

God is creating you as a loving, sexual, bodily being. Whatever your singular mix and measure of sexuality, be glad: to be a human sexual is 'fundamental and ordinary and exceptional' *[Iris Murdoch]*.

25

Because you are loved unconditionally, you do not have to take yourself too seriously. If you were the finger of God, and all the world was ticklish . . .

26

If you are wounded 'in the groin', shocked into rigidity, let yourself breathe gently, allow the warmth to bring you alive again, but slowly, neither complaining about the ache nor expecting sudden healing.

27

Then dare to ask for different moments of bodily loving from someone you trust: small healing sacraments of touch, where loneliness is relieved, delight is shared, flesh is comforted, and sleep is trusted.

28

At times, though, all you can do is cleave to hope, loyally bearing the wounds, gently probing them, living and delving the space between yourself and another: and the touch of a finger tip will be enough.

MARCH

1

For Lige Clarke and Jack Nichols, the most loving sexual act of all is gently to reach for another and through touch make that person feel whole.

2

Human beings have always drawn boundaries between clean and dirty. But ask this: After making love, do you feel you need a bath or that you have had a bath?

3

When fear comes, speak the fear, feel the fear, breathe into the fear, move gently out of your rigidity, picture the ice round your heart melting in the sun, laugh . . . The Presence is very close, very loving . . .

4

Do not forgive too easily or too soon. Certainly let the hurt be warmed into compassion not frozen into bitterness, but you may need to wait for a sign of repentance if reconciliation is to be real.

5

Can you, without blanching, look directly into the eye of the one you have hurt and humbly ask to be forgiven? Can you receive from the one who is refusing to retaliate? Can you bear the cost?

6

To receive forgiveness is to let go of your controlling, self-justifying, surface self. It is the only way to life. And to let go in small ways is to prepare for the final letting go, for the decisive moment of truth.

7

To be destitute, deprived, oppressed, enslaved is to be totally trapped, with no power to influence events. To be saved is to be enlarged, to be free to roam in wide open spaces, with room to wrestle with the enemy.

8

Love your enemies. Do not condemn them, do not 'damn' them in your turn, do not seek to enslave them or destroy them. Keep in contact, even if you cannot 'keep in touch'.

9

Strive powerfully with your enemies, struggle with them shoulder to shoulder, and be surprised when you see each other face to face. Do not yield to bitterness or despair, to violence or violation: but *struggle*.

10

Do not demonize even your worst enemies, stigmatizing them as subhuman, thus giving yourself permission to maim and kill. Be angry if need be, but let compassion, not hatred, be felt through your anger.

11

Dissolve the hatred by recognizing within yourself how much you have learned to hate yourself, internalizing harmful messages from long ago. Believe rather, deep in your heart, that *you are totally loved*.

12

At the same time, and for the time being, you may need to protect yourself. Do not throw pearls before swine, and while being as vulnerable as you dare, do not be a doormat to be trampled on.

13

Look also for opportunities to tell your story, for argument never won over an enemy, and your courage in being vulnerable will at least impress and sometimes silence and make thoughtful those who hear.

14

Be powerfully and persuasively gentle, with others and with yourself. Stand (on) your own ground with dignity. And keep a sense of proportion – and above all a sense of humour.

15

If you are a stiff-necked burden-shoulderer, let Love guide your embodied being, let Spirit flow through you, and let the government be on God's shoulders, not your own.

16

Hold on to your life – lose it. Let go of your life – find it. Let go. Let be. Let God. Be rooted and grounded in the Love that is the Ground of your being. Be drawn by the Love that is the Goal of your becoming.

17

A character in Nikos Kazantzakis' novel about St Francis, *God's Pauper*, says of the 'larva' that dwells within each of us: 'Lean over and say to this larva, I love you, and it will sprout wings and become a butterfly.'

18

William Blake wrote, 'We are on this earth that we may learn to bear the beams of love.' Pierre Teilhard de Chardin echoes that: 'Only so can our love for others be a burning gentleness.'

19

Aelred of Rievaulx wrote: 'If you have no love of your own lasting interest, if you hate your own soul (and show it by loving evil), how can you love the very being, the deepest interests, of another?'

20

Kierkegaard wrote: 'Do not despair, never give up hope for yourself or for one another. Bitter enemies and lost friends can become friends again. Love that has grown cold can kindle and burst into flame.'

21

Be content with the impossibilities, the incompletions, from within which alone the future is given shape and meaning. Listen to the whisper of the thunder on a distant shore.

22

Your comprehensive task is to be a human being whose depths are divine. 'Look for the sunlight in your wood and stone, look for the skygod in your flesh and bone.'

23

If biology is not destiny, may you be drawn beyond the past and beyond the present, into what is greater and larger, an as yet unimagined whole that is far more than the sum of the parts.

24

Pierre Teilhard de Chardin thought that 'spiritual fecundity' would more and more accompany the 'material fecundity' of procreation and would ultimately become the sole reason for sexual union.

25

Arthur Miller believed that every human being shows courage in facing one or another challenge or conflict. If we knew what it was, we would be full of admiration.

26

A mystery story is a puzzle that can be solved, a mystery tour takes you to a place that will be revealed when you get there, but there is the profounder mystery that can be delved but proves to be inexhaustible.

27

The patient, persistent pressures exerted by non-violent actions may protect the integrity of the peacemakers, but they can protect nothing more. Who bears the cost of the pressures we exert?

28

To 'come out' is to emerge into the light of day, to come out to play, openly to be a human sexual, of however peculiar a kind, to be life-affirming, visible, reaching out to connect with others.

29

There is another kind of 'coming out', which is to be separate, to shout into the wind, with nobody listening, nobody hearing the story, nobody in conversation. It is to be fanatical, sectarian, loveless.

30

If you live under the shadow of a stigma, dismissed by category rather than discerned by character, you are open to the hidden gift that everything that is good comes to you unearned, as grace.

31

Aim not for success or status, but for a life that becomes a sign of salvation to the rejected. Do not become unavailable to them by becoming acceptable to those who do not like their comfort disturbed. *[After Mother Jane SLG]*

APRIL

1

Our ancestors gave much in striving to make their world more just, their descendants enjoying the fruits of their struggles. Be grateful for them and in your turn make sacrifices for the sake of the future.

2

When a life-giving place becomes death-dealing, stretch forward, shoulders aching, through yet another dark tunnel, another narrow gate, into a wide open space where you can again breathe freely.

3

Relish chores. Do not talk or drive fast. Slow down. Next time you are *running* late, *walk*. Next time you are thinking through a problem, or trying to make a decision, *wait* for the *second* clarity. *[After F. von Hügel]*

4

When tempted to *react* quickly, pause, step back, breathe gently, stand in your own place on your own feet, see the other who may have power over you as truly other. Then – and only then – *respond*.

5

Do not deny your own strengths through false modesty or self-abasement. Gentleness is strength refined and chan- nelled, not denied or concealed.

6

If you pretend you have no strengths, you will swing be- tween sentimentality and cruelty, two sides of the same coin. And others will be afraid of you and bewildered by you.

7

Do not depend on institutions for permission or approval or a ready-made role. Sense your own ground and dignity and strength, and make your singular contribution from that ground.

8

Even if you are an ordinary member of an organization, you are part of it. It is an 'us', not an 'us and them'. You can help guide its future with wisdom and compassion and creative energy.

9

Being made in the divine image, unable to escape the divine presence, both you and me, each of us is of absolute significance to the other, and none of us can be a mere means to an end.

10

I love you because you are you and because I love God who is in you. I cannot love you as a by-product of my love for God, for I am loving God when I love you. Like God, I am committed to you for ever.

11

Do you let yourself 'go through' your experience? Or are you 'not all there'? We can be content only if full of content – or when we are content to be empty.

12

Let the ice melt from around your heart. Let the running water, at first only a trickle, melt the icicles of your heart's winter, sharp and frozen fear relaxing into warm and flowing tears.

13

Say Yes to a love that will drag you through the depths, illuminate your every darkness, scour your every feeling, scar and heal your heart, lift you to the heights.

14

You have loved and lost. Do not cling. Accept the separa-
tion, the distance, for the sake of an unknown impossible
future, a 'resurrection from the dead', unpredictable but
inevitable – at the right time.

15

Seek contact – not too much or you will be drained; withdrawal – not too much or you will be frozen; attention
– not too much or you will be smothered; aloneness – not
too much or you will be isolated.

16

You loosen your clothing to shit, to pray, to roar, to love,
to sleep. The belly needs room to move and relax. The Bible
talks of 'the bowels of compassion'. You can't be compassionate if you're constipated.

17

Let go of your 'up-tight-ness': only then can you give – in
or out. Don't hold your breath. Breathe far out, trusting
the air will be there to rush in. Hold on to your life – lose
it. Let go of your life – save it.

18

'I feel completely safe in your arms.' 'I bet you will do anything I want.' An exchange of safety for control. What is
missing is risk. Risk is the companion of faith and adventure and growth.

19

Ask what is legitimately private and what is acceptably public. Bring into the public domain what you have learned in private, but find a way of doing so that does not betray that privacy.

20

When you wrestle with meaning, whether the angel you strive with is in your dreams or incarnate in your neighbour, find a shape by which to communicate to others what you have learned.

21

If you refuse the challenge of the next step, you may be safe, but you will have chilled your inner being by a degree. Risk hurt and failure, be vulnerable, take courage. Then you will be creative and grow.

22

Neither of us is God, whose love is unlimited. You are not totally dependable and reliable, I am not totally courageous and compassionate. Dare we risk loving each other, come what may?

23

Wounds always leave their mark, physical scars visible on the skin, emotional hurts trapped in cell and muscle. Gently but firmly, accurate touch will bring a groan of release and a measure of healing.

24

Are you a peacemaker in the politics of the everyday, in family and community? The conflicts may be less dramatic than those in the headlines, but they reveal the same human distress and dislocation.

25

If we work gently, firmly, consistently, persistently, patiently, at the making of peace, we may reach 'critical mass' and be helping forward a mutation in the corporate consciousness of humankind.

26

Carefully and thoughtfully explore the big questions, even though you cannot find the answers. The answers come as a gift, unexpectedly, unpredictably, and provoke the question, Where did that come from?

27

If you have no words to express what you feel, if you have not learned 'your own language', and if you are not heard, your frustration will increase: you will either hit out in fury or hate yourself into despair.

28

Trust in the memory of your best moments, of the stories that matter. Then you will be faithful in your worst moments, and trust that what is coming in the future will work out for your greater good. That is faith.

29

'God' is greater than you, an ocean to your wave. But you too are greater than the sum of your parts. 'God' is more than the sum of all of us. And through our loving 'God' is growing all the time.

30

'God' is the past within us, source of our being. 'God' is the present among us, invisibly at work, usually unrecognized. 'God' is the future beyond us, luring, beckoning, yearning.

MAY

1

Love allows time for *nothing* to happen. Resist the temptation to fill the emptiness, for even the undoubtedly good may be the enemy of the unpredictably good, and the immediate may squeeze out the vital.

2

Do not cling to the Parent who gave you new birth. Taking leave of God is as much part of a maturing faith as coming home to God. A sense of absence is as nurturing as a sense of presence.

3

You may not matter to each other more than any*thing* else in the world, or more than any*one* else in the world, but the way in which you matter to each other is irreplaceable, and that matters very much indeed.

4

Because the void, opened by unrequited love, cannot be filled, you are challenged to live *within* and *from* that void, bearing the ache of ever-deepening love for the other and for everybody else in your life.

5

God is not a painkiller, cheaply filling the void. But by living from the centre and depth of the void, the divine love will grow *in* you, and come to be expressed *through* you. Simply keep open your aching heart.

6

To fall in love is to bow down to an idol. It is a delight, no doubt, but also a lie. The other cannot meet all your needs. The other is not perfect. Life is not this simple. Your problems are not solved. Wake up.

7

The truth-in-love is honest about disappointment and anger, muddles and perplexity. Only the love that is prolonged and sustained can contain and transform the energies unleashed by falling in love.

8

Let there be space between you. Remember that the ones you hold close to your heart are but guests in the deep places of your being. There may be clamour to be cleared before music is heard.

9

Recognize that to be fully human you need both chores and creativity. At the heart of every simple repeated task is the call to attention and detail, without which detail the creative cannot take shape.

10

Be a nonsense, a symbol of that which does not fit in. (Does evolution depend on the survival not only of the fittest, which may not be the strongest, but also of what has not yet been recognized as fit?)

11

A project, a job, a chapter of your life – each has its dawning, noon, and afternoon If you do not move on when the time is ripe, the advancing shadows will spread their murk, and you lose your way.

12

The jewel of wealth and display may signify a great love, but makes its owner vulnerable to attack and adds to the income of insurers. The jewel of sunlight piercing the mist cannot be grasped or stolen.

13

Enjoy the shaft of sunlight, the scent of a summer evening, the smile of a child, a simple act of kindness. Even enjoy a moment of praise. But don't inhale. *[After Basil Hume]*

14

Tensions pull you in different directions. Stand your ground. Drop your centre of gravity. Become aware of a deeper desire deep down. Let the energy well up that can contain and move the tensions.

15

You may not act violently, but you may still be violating others: manipulating, stigmatizing, withholding warmth and affection, stunning others with looks or wealth, holding back your humanity.

16

In Dante's *Inferno* the courtesans are in the same place as the forgers. Both deal in counterfeit. They easily disrupt, confuse, block the flow of true love and devalue true coinage.

17

To go through a narrow gate is to accept constriction, restraint, limitation. There is only one way left, your unique path, and it will always include a measure of dying. There is no way back.

18

Give yourself to a task that is greater than you are, that will always defeat you. Put all your energy into it, spend it until there is nothing left. Then you will die having lived.

19

Disagree by all means, but do not reject. Do not push away or draw back. Receive the other as other, and so also be received. For you need the other in order to discover what you do not yet know about yourself.

20

When you are engaged on a task you have not allowed enough time for, you hurry and half your mind is on what you will be late for and only half on the task before you. You are elsewhere rather than here.

21

To succumb to 'accidie' is to become lazy, sullen, morbid, hard-hearted, self-centred. Its opposite is 'com*punc*tion', a '*punc*turing' of the balloon of false self, a piercing of the heart, a cutting to the quick.

22

To counter accidie, do some simple physical work, phone a neighbour, remember you may die tonight, *intend* to change if you do not have the *desire* to do so, keep on praying and moving – gently.

23

The mystic sense (or non-sense) of God: no-thing because of whom there is every-thing, no-one because of whom there is every-one, an emptiness in which to dance, an abyss down which to soar.

24

Are you the devourer who needs to move away from the other so as to inhabit your own at present troubled space, or are you the fearful who needs to move towards the other in order to learn to trust and receive?

25

Still the whirring wings of your thoughts, the ceaseless buzzing round your brain. Fold the wings across your chest, that your heart may be warmed and hatched.

26

Pray your way into the constrictions of your cell until you know it as a place of freedom. Close your door willingly before the door is closed upon you. So learn to trust the final cell that will be your death bed.

27

For Rilke, the artist is a dancer whose movements are broken against the walls of a cell. He bids the dancer: stretch the unlived lines of your body into the walls with your wounded fingers.

28

If you find it hard to trust, you will need to learn to let go of your hard-won control and fall into what looks like a bottomless pit of terror but is in truth an unfathomable abyss of love.

29

Let your touch be gentle, warm, not tightly but lightly holding. Let it be leisurely and lingering. Let it be discerning, honest, genuine. Let it flow outwards from the centre of your being, from the place of truth . . .

30

. . . So let your touch come from the diffusion of loving energy throughout the flesh-body. In these ways your touch will be the divinely given and divinely charged means of reaching out and drawing close.

31

You cannot tell your secrets, the hidden stories, without making yourself vulnerable, at the mercy of the other. But if you do not tell your story, your life is washed away, faded and forgotten.

JUNE

1

Though each lives alone, there is a world of difference between the recluse who hates humankind, having nothing to do with others, and the hermit who loves humankind, praying in solidarity with others.

2

The more you are truly yourself, the less power you will have over others, the more you will be content to share power with others, and the more you will be prepared for the rest to be taken away.

3

The more you refuse the burden of your own struggle, the weightier will be the burden that others have to bear. And if you bear the burden *in* 'God', the yoke will be easy, the burden light.

4

If someone is a burden to you, focus on your *will* to love, and on the fact of the other being human like you, and think of that exercise as training you in learning to love someone who really has harmed you.

5

However you relate to others, with your own power or as part of an organization or society, you will oppress them when that power *systematically* imposes burdens on those less powerful than you are.

6

If you talk of someone as 'not quite one of us', or you think of someone as not quite as fully human as you are, you are on the slippery path that can lead to the concentration camp.

7

Never refer to 'ethnic *cleansing*': it is ethnic *slaughter*, however much it feels as if you are 'wiping the slate clean'. Be glad that you are unclean, impure, that we are all mixed up. We're all mongrels. Alleluia!

8

The opposite of the harmonious and well ordered is the chaotic and dis-ordered, not the wild and untamed. They have their own reasons – as does the human heart.

9

No place is now untouched by humans. Even the wilderness receives radiation on the wind, electronic pulses from satellites, and changing weather patterns from global warming. A presence for good or ill?

10

Grounded in Being, a wave in the Ocean, you are paradoxically addressed, called, lured, courteously but irresistibly, by One who is like a true lover. All-is-One, *and* I-and-Thou.

11

Ask if and how you believe in life beyond death? The total shedding of your false self and the continuing identity (of which you may not yet even be aware) of your true self? . . .

12

. . . But put that belief in your attic, lest you cease to care for the earth, lest you do not learn how to die by living fully now, lest you use religion as drug or prop, lest you avoid the impact of desolation.

13

Groucho Marx said he would prefer heaven for the climate but hell for the company. But if hell is the awareness of being separated from Love, is it ever beyond the reach of Love?

14

Do not walk away from an awkward question but walk along with it, holding it and bearing it, persistently and gently delving it. That is what it means to walk in a sacred manner.

15

The murmuring of your unresolved distress, and the thundering of the pain of others: can you weave these discords with notes of joy, so as to make melodies more profound than any we have yet heard?

16

Your relationship with human beings is not secondary to your relationship with God. But recognize that it is indeed *God* you encounter *through* those relationships – if they are truthful and loving.

17

It is one of life's sorrows that only rarely do we find ourselves able to rest secure in the heart of another. Yet those moments are samples of what it is to rest in God, without whom we are for ever restless.

18

Love, sleep and truth resent too direct an approach. Tell your story indirectly and tactfully. The 'naked' truth can be subtly erotic, but it can also be blatantly pornographic.

19

If you throw yourself away, or you throw yourself at another, you will disintegrate. If you give yourself away, or you give yourself to another, you will become integrated.

20

Force your way and nothing real will come your way. Wait. Look. Listen. Love the distance between desire and fulfilment. What you need will be given, if you truly desire it, but always to your surprise.

21

Let the seed germinate. Give it its own time, gently water it from time to time, and be patient. You will not recognize the flower until it opens. To dig and dissect is to destroy.

22

Parasites, devourers, bludgeoners, complainers, grating voices, flutterers, the twitterers, loud voices? Tough: they are your sacred guests, jewels hidden in the mud you splatter them with.

23

To create what is new entails a measure of loneliness. Bear the discomfort, lower yourself gently into it, inhabit it, and discover at its heart a greater ease and the spacious freedom of solitude.

24

To define scriptures, creeds, doctrines as the final word is to close yourself to life. Moisture and spirit seep away and you are left with a dry husk. The Spirit seeks new forms in and through us, here and now.

25

Without mercy, you are cold. No mercy, no 'merci' – no gratitude. Also no 'merc-hant', no 'com-merce', no capacity for the kind of exchange by which both parties benefit. You are left only with power.

26

Rilke claimed that it is at times of perplexity that something new, unknown, as yet unrecognized, enters your being, to begin a work of transformation, something that will in time prove crucial to your life.

27

The dark angel that brings you anxiety, sleeplessness, threat, even terror, may, once recognized, be helpless, needing your compassion and bearing gifts you need, ready to be your ally and protector.

28

You *are* dearly loved. You *are* of infinite worth. You *are* marvellous and wonderful. The Voice within says, 'I take great delight in you.' And it is only when you forget these truths that life goes awry.

29

Wait like the birdwatcher, silent, attentive, for whoever and whatever is approaching to reveal itself. Great art, holy people, divine mystery: their presence transforms – if you give of yourself *into* that attention.

30

The more you claim to be righteous, the more you are likely to be unaware of a desire to punish. The more you deny your hidden negative desires, the more you hate yourself.

JULY

1

You are a node in an interconnecting web of power, you make an explicit or implicit contribution to systems that treat some human beings as inferior, at worst as inhuman, and therefore expendable.

2

Be quietly attentive to what is happening within you and within the other, and allow the truth to show itself between you. Be midwives to each other's struggle and hope in the birthing of new life.

3

Detach yourself from everything you project on to others, so that you may see them as they truly are. Clear your eyes that your vision may be luminous, without fantasy or delusion.

4

Your besetting, repeated wrongdoings are the obscure gateway to the love which humbles you by accepting you again and again, and will not humiliate you or condemn you as you condemn yourself.

5

In the dark tunnel learn to find your way by touch, adjust to what you cannot see if there is too much light, make the darkness your home, dwell there, keep faith. You need not be stuck: keep moving gently.

6

To be given a vision is not unusual. To live it out is rare. The shaping of a vision is usually to organize it so much that it is stifled. The vision is your glory, the betrayal is your tragedy.

7

Let tears soften the limescale of your being, refresh your shrivelled heart, still your agitated mind, clear the eye of your perception. Then you can will the one thing needful that next you need to do.

8

If you know more than you can embody, you have to learn by suffering that enough is enough. If you demand too much of yourself, suffering will come your way to teach you that you have limitations.

9

'Soul' is your deep self under the movement of pressure, not least the pressure of your pain and contradictions, which at best evoke trust in a greater power keeping you moving in the right direction.

10

Be content with a divided mind, for the precise mind, with-out doubt or indecision, persecutes. Be content with a sense of failure, for success puts you above others, and seduces you into ideologies. *[Graham Greene]*

10

Be content with an uneasy conscience, for the supposedly guiltless conscience scapegoats and commits atrocities with an easy mind. *[Graham Greene]*

11

Wake up from the delusions of your surface self – from Adonises to alcohol – for even what is natural and good misleads if it becomes the only good in your life.

12

Do you prefer to remain in prison, not actually wanting to be rescued? Do you prefer to be ruined than to change, to 'die in your dread' rather than 'see your illusions die'? *[W. H. Auden]*

13

Necessity is that which cannot be changed. It is near neigh-bour to short-term living, to compulsion, addiction, debili-tating habits. Vocation is the call to transform necessity, a long-term task.

14

Desire the impossible, *desire* to grow in love, but do not *try* to force anything. Stretch yourself into the measure of what cannot yet be, letting your cry fill your being but not overwhelm it.

15

Be dedicated to whoever or whatever is other than you and greater than you, and do not begrudge the chores and the routines which give shape to that dedication.

16

Let the inner work, the personal journey, the *heart*-work, let them blend with the outer work of making connections with others, in the networks of affection, concern, hard work, always weaving and mending.

17

Friendship cannot be true and lasting until it has lived through the questions of how to love the space, the yawning gaps, between you, and how to keep in touch when you have wounded each other.

18

In the rift of your heart, hidden in your wounded side, my heartbreak finds a home. In the rift of my heart you choose to set up the tent of your dwelling.

19

Let your heart burn with love for the whole of creation, for men and women and children, for the birds, the beasts and the demons. Radiate a fleshly warmth in compassion and tender care. *[Isaac the Syrian]*

20

From the unravelling cloth, let go of the threads that dis-integrate, dye the resilient ones afresh, spin new ones. Try out a small tentative design. Pass it on, at a turn in time, to the weavers now being born.

21

Be a body 'en-spirited', be a body 'im-passioned'. For it is never passion that is the source of evil, but an envious eye, a hard heart, a callous body.

22

When you are disintegrating into fragments, cherish the pieces of faded mosaic for new patterns you do not yet discern: even fragments can be gathered, whether of stone or bread.

23

To be virgin is to be continuously open, to keep available a space into which you can invite another, even one who will cause you pain, that there may be a new birth – again and again.

24

In the crisis through which the world is passing, when many *fall* by the wayside, perhaps the only choice we have is *how* we fall, resistant, rebellious, afraid, or welcoming, obedient, trusting.

25

The *grip* of evil: the inordinate rather than the balanced; the delusory rather than the truthful; the solemn rather than the light-hearted; the frozen rather than the warm-hearted.

26

To be gripped by evil is to be held fast by the reflection in a mirror of distortions. Their names are many: revenge, malice, greed, hatred; the small impulsive hardly noticed deeds that trigger tragedy.

27

Think of the *net* of evil, in which we are together enmeshed, more powerful than the sum of individual actions, loosened only by truth, humility, compassion, forgiveness, laughter.

28

Original sin is a pervasive disorientation whereby life is *organized* for decay, disaster, destruction, deadliness. We deeply desire doom and disintegration, *en-thralled* when we see it on the screen.

29

Let yourself be lured into the wilderness, drawn into the desert by an invisible but powerful thread, so that there the Other may speak to your heart. *[After Hosea 2.14]*

30

Be recollected, gathered together, totally present, mind-full, care-full, in each particular of daily life. Only so can you live that life in its abundance and *full*ness. (And its opposite is irreligious . . .)

31

As a pilgrim, which is more important to you, the destination or the journey, the accomplishment or the awareness? Are you hurrying by the clock or sauntering by the sun? Is it more like work or like play?

AUGUST

1

Do you choose 'absurdity' (from *ab surdus*, 'completely deaf') or 'obedience' (from *ab audiens,* 'listening with the heart attuned to the deepest meaning')? The more you listen, the more you are silent.

2

In contemplation you are 'given over' to loving and patient attention to what is. *From* contemplation, you 'give yourself over' to passionate engagement with what is given. In both you 'empty yourself' in trust.

3

As a 'hermit', as a 'prophet', as a 'monk' pioneering the Way, as a 'fool' dancing on the edge, you need a 'bishop' to keep an eye on the whole, 'over-seeing', to hold you and others together.

4

You need a 'bishop' to guard your boundaries, to keep the bullies and persecutors at bay, and to help and encourage you in hard times, so enhancing and not restricting your freedom.

5

At its best, authority is not that which frustrates you and against which you chafe, but a wise proviso for recognizing human limitations and enabling human flourishing.

6

Self-conscious about prayer, you will become pious and priggish. God-conscious about life, you will become de-voted and delightful. Close enough *to* God, you will know how to keep quiet *about* God.

7

The most powerful and shielded are the most isolated, the least available for love, above themselves, with the fur-thest to fall. On a fragile planet they are the least fit for survival.

8

If you live on your own, you may well feel lonely when the last guest has departed. Ease yourself gently into the loneliness and in time a rich solitude will open within you. *[After May Sarton]*

9

Do not fret about feeling unfulfilled, incomplete. Accept it, and allow a fruitfulness to grow in you unknown and unseen. The only way you can stop that process is to try and understand it. *[After Thomas Merton]*

10

To choose well is to say a wholehearted No (even to what is good) for the sake of a more wholehearted Yes (to a greater good) without knowing in advance what that Yes will entail.

11

Detach yourself from the busy-ness of too many commitments, however justifiable each may be. By no longer dispersing energy, you can go deep enough to be gathered into a profound unity of being.

12

Drop your weight into the ground of your being, let yourself be enfolded by the mysterious presence, and only then let the firm yet gentle energy rise up and flow into whatever you are required to do.

13

Walk gently, slowing down, aware of silence, presence, being, mystery, 'sauntering' to your 'sainte terre', your 'holy land', moving more deeply into the sacredness of here and now.

14

Enjoy the child in you, who exults in wild and empty places, who ventures eagerly to see what is round the next cor-
ner, the child who is lithe, graceful, and at home here and
now, by name, Laughing Water.

15

The truly spiritual is not more airy, but more rooted. Our
destiny is not to be wispy ghosts but transformed bodies.
C. S. Lewis described Narnia as a '*deeper* country', and
Charles Wesley wrote of '*solid* joys'.

16

You feel isolated, dismayed, in pain, bearing a secret burden, ashamed, stigmatized: recall the *reality* (even if you
are unaware) that you are connected with everybody and
everything, always and everywhere.

17

Are you actually free when you are doing what you want
to do, or when you truly want to do what you most deeply
believe you must? Can you obey destiny with delight?

18

Here and there, you become aware that the place where
you tread is sacred ground. When you are aware that the
place where you tread is far from being sacred ground,
your task is to make it so.

19

It is easy to speak in ways that will not harm you, dreaming of applause and wealth, your fear and vanity staining your work. Only if you are empty enough will you find the voice that is most truly yours.

20

Stuff accumulates. Clear the clutter. Too much comes in. Too little is digested. Organize your home that more goes out than comes in. Don't let things choke the life and movement out of you.

21

Examine your motives for caring for others. Guilt about an easy life? A need to be liked? Genuine compassion? Does your badge read, 'I'll give you all the help I need?'

22

You are not always available for others. You need to sleep, eat and play – especially if you have no partner or children to bring you down to earth.

23

Be realistic about how available you are. Set boundaries: you can ignore them in an emergency. (Surely your life is not one long emergency?)

24

And take time to be alone, locked against all intrusion – time to become acquainted and at ease with yourself, time to focus on the One, however mysterious, hidden and seemingly absent.

25

To be attached is to mix demand and gift, never entirely selfless. To be detached is to give freedom to the other. Wean yourself from attachment, not because you are indifferent, but because you love.

26

If you put yourself before the Work, neither you nor it will last. If you put the Work before yourself, both will endure (though it be at the cost of enduring . . .). Let the Work be the servant of your maturing.

27

The Work will, however, constantly defeat you because it is greater than you. You will never completely be 'up to it'. But from such defeats you will learn and grow.

28

Among your many voices discern your own true voice. That voice is singular, unique to you. Give it your attention and your skill. But let the Music, which does not belong to you, sing through that voice.

29

If you can dare to be different, dare to be your unique self, you will be both lonely and at home. You are being created with particular care. Whether others accept you is neither here nor there.

30

The deeper your work, the fewer will be your con-tacts, 'in-touch-with' you. A profound resonance is possible only with a few, be they words, pictures, melodies, people. And the silence and the solitude will grow.

31

Places of 'birth' need boundaries, excluding none who seek what they can give, but exclusive in protecting their special purpose. They need 'guardians' set apart to serve them (though never separate or 'above').

SEPTEMBER

1

Sexual energy can fuel release and pleasure, comfort and healing, the conceiving of a child or the sustaining of a human love – and, when the flames glow rather than sparkle, a deeper, divine creativity.

2

You bump against your limits, and within them there will always be something unfulfilled. You cry out from the emptiness. This is the moment to *warm* to the impossible.

3

The rueful wonder will dawn on you that it is precisely from what you have found impossible that you will free others to live what you cannot. Then your sense of limitations and emptiness will lose its bitterness.

4

Pick up an object at random. Is it practically useful, emotionally nourishing, spiritually helpful? If not, pass it on. Recycle it, sell it, give it away.

5

Less clutter – more simplicity – more conviviality. Less clatter – more silence – more conversation. Less chatter – more solitude – more communion. But the things, words and people that remain do *matter.*

6

Fully aware, clear within, open to others, intimately at one with the Source of being, free of entanglements, your simple presence, your few words, your accurate touch, will transmit life and will liberate. *[So John V. Taylor understood the presence of Jesus.]*

7

If my life is not entangled in your pain, I can absorb that pain without its poisoning me. My energy will ebb as I do so, but all I need to do is simply to wait for the tide to turn, and the flow will re-charge me.

8

I receive and ground your pain. You receive and are lifted by my hope. (Or the other way round.) Both of us exchange life and touch joy. Pain has been absorbed and hostility neutralized.

9

Because we are rarely completely free from our own and others' entanglements, such healing exchanges need bathing in the Spirit of the One who is pure, unbounded Love.

10

Until you burn your boat, ending a chapter of your life, with no way of return, as long as you hesitate, you are divided within. You can still draw back, exchanging adventure for security.

11

When you do let go, 'Providence' also moves, moves towards you with unexpected gifts. 'Events' seem to 'happen'. Encounters surprise you with what you need. None of it could you have 'dreamt up'.

12

'Come out' as your true self, saved from despair, set free from imprisonment, no longer prone to self-hatred and foul temper, no longer 'prey' to lies: at peace, empowered, full of energy.

13

You can never *solve* a fundamental problem, trying to work it out as if it were a puzzle with a correct solution. What is unresolved is not 'soluble', cannot be 'dis-solved'. It can only be outgrown. *[Carl Jung]*

14

Are those with whom you network part of a burgeoning earth-saving community or merely a spiritual and material elite? It is the old question: Are you chosen for privilege and power or for service?

15

When your surface streams run dry, you need to withdraw energy from outer things and patiently cherish your inner being, however far underground, however silent the water, letting it amass for a new day. *[After Laurens van der Post]*

16

Beware the ancient desire to conform, whether to blue jeans or to blue rinse, to fascism or communism, mirroring identical cancerous cells, monoculture replacing biodiversity. The desert warns.

17

Treat your problem as your problem *child*. Reverence your child, however problematic. Your child, cherished, attended to, quietened, will lead you to your deep true being, and enlarge your heart.

18

Contribute to a cairn, (a stone costs no money), and so mark a memorable event or person, a path through difficult territory, an encounter, a revelation, a turning point – however unlikely the place.

19

When sorrow finds a name and a voice, it is like the lightning you see calling and the thunder speaking after it to say that soon the rains will fall on you again. *[A bushman of the Kalahari Desert]*

20

Bring probing mind, loving heart, and imagination to bear upon what you 'take in'. So you will digest it, using its energy without its turning sour. Beware what can turn on you and devour you.

21

If you want to change somebody, you won't do it by argument or force or by demanding something impossible. Your only chance is to be something irresistible. *[After May Sarton]*

22

In the darkness of fanaticism, cherish thoughtfulness, mongrels, art, tenderness, beautiful land and buildings, books, intimacy, trust, and the guardians, the lawkeepers, the peacemakers. *[After May Sarton]*

23

Ask those who have died before you to make love more wholeheartedly than they ever did in this life, so that their love-making, now more true, accurate and engodded, may overflow to your good.

24

Are you still vulnerable to being pulled out of orbit by sudden, powerful, compulsive attraction? How far are you able to enjoy without needing to possess or be possessed?

25

Carry through the thrust of energy and rise to meet it, but at the right moment, without either premature spurt and yearning, or withdrawal and collapse. Let build. Follow through. Only when ripe, let go.

26

You will not find yourself by looking in a mirror or by hunting some elusive 'self', but by contemplating what is, and by accepting a discipline and routine which keeps you engaged with what is.

27

Enjoy your poor memory: you can't be a good liar, you can't tell long stories, you forget offences, and you enjoy places and books a second time. (There may be a fifth benefit: I've forgotten.) *[After Montaigne]*

28

Cherish the friend to whom you can pour out the contents of your heart, grain and chaff, knowing that the gentlest of hands will sift it, keeping what is of worth and with kindness blow the rest away. *[Arab proverb]*

29

If you give yourself to others, you put yourself in their power, at their mercy. You are at your most vulnerable, and you do not know in advance whether their mercies will be tender mercies.

30

When you are challenged to give up some security, wealth, position, you prefer others to change rather than yourself. Rather than be 'trans-formed' you 'trans-fer' unwelcome change on to others.

OCTOBER

1

Be gently firm, enduringly patient, and quietly wise enough to live with a problem without knowing the solution. It can't be given by means of what you already know. Wait for a gift and a surprise.

2

You cannot know yourself on your own. It is only by revealing yourself to another that the truth emerges, for the deepest truth involves the challenges of love – and that demands courage.

3

Mature virginity is a state of continuing openness, a willingness to greet whoever and whatever calls, to be impregnated whenever and wherever 'the other' draws close.

4

To be 'ever virgin' is always to be on the threshold, open to divine exploration, to become an explorer of virgin territory, and an embodier of the Mysterious Unknown.

5

Your calling may be to make your home on the threshold, committed to whatever is coming to be, ready to welcome others when they approach their thresholds and help them across and beyond.

6

Your beautiful wilderness, vulnerable to intrusion, your creative child self, needs your adult care and parenting boundaries, so that you can say No to those who think you can satisfy their unquenchable thirst.

7

Let the gate to your true being neither swing open with every breeze nor seize up with rust. Always open, you give the message of unsatisfied need, always closed, you give the message of severe wound.

8

Are your actions sporadic, dis-connected, momentary, inconsequential? Or are they repeated, connected, enduring, effective? Are you *base*-less or well-*ground*ed? Living fatally or fate-fully?

9

Do not hate yourself and destroy yourself. Love yourself and nourish yourself. Reverence the Self that is coming to be, taking shape from deep within. Only then can you reverence others and all creation. *[After Sogyal Rinpoche]*

10

Welcome the ebb tide. Welcome the longer nights as autumn falls. The time may feel grey and drear, but replenishment comes with it as you rest. Be gentle with yourself: to force the pace is to collapse.

11

Imagine a compassionate face. Look at it quietly. Take the image to yourself, at one with your own face. Turn the look outwards, towards others. Then *act* kindly. So the Compassionate One lives through you.

12

Solitude (not isolated, not reclusive) is creative only if it is a way of love, in a world of bodies, where you touch and are touched, not yielding to possession, but yearning with compassion.

13

To be, as the old hymn has it, 'hidden in your wounded side', is to be close, very near, absorbing the throbbing of heartlove, the pulsing of lifeblood, and the spreading ecstasy of the loins.

14

Keep your sense of direction (physical) and your sense of direction (spiritual). Keep your eyes on the goal. But not too rigidly – or you will miss something vital at your feet.

15

Oracles are always ambivalent. What is nourishment to one person may well be poison to another. What is nourishment at one stage of life may well be poison at another.

16

Non-possessive love gives and receives delight and pleasure, creates varied and complex phenomena, imagines the hospitable love of the Three-in-One, richer and deeper and more *sexual* than we realize.

17

To be committed, to will one thing, to burn boats: Is this a confinement or a refinement? To be purified is to know the dross of self burnt, and the flame of self-giving bright. [After Sr Madeleine]

18

The threads of text and email, postcards and letters, are slender, and, being disembodied, need the occasions of sight and hearing and, above all, touch, sacrament of the living mystery of love.

19

What is your sense of body and place (including churches)? Dense, pea-soupy, dark, thick grey, entrapping, compulsively skewed, or solid, dancing, light, multi-coloured, freeing, calmly centred?

20

Wise authority does not expect others always to get it right, but does ask you challenging questions, and is ready to explore them with you, discerning from what is difficult the possibilities of new growth.

21

The heart of the matter? At heart? Heart-rending, heart-broken, heartfelt, losing your heart, taking to heart, with all your heart, whole-hearted, light-hearted, heartening, take heart – for love's sake.

22

Scent the track of the G** who has disappeared over the horizon. Listen for the Dream, the Story, the Coming, that will meet the needs of our desperate global day. Listen for the trickle in the parched valley.

23

Provisional law says,
Your best will be loved; your worst will be judged.
Necessary gospel says,
Your best will be judged; your worst will be loved.

24

Beware when others speak well of you. If anyone sings your praises, ask what went wrong with the lyric or the tune, or both. And remember that birds of prey sing no songs.

25

Gather. Listen. Scribble. Wait. Listen. Write. Wait. Look at what you have written. Where did all that come from? You are astonished. You don't know how 'it' happened. And it draws from you obedience.

26

You have memories of wounding touch. You cannot trust that tender touch is real. Let the fear melt gently. Otherwise, seized up, you cannot change, you cannot come alive, you cannot know true love.

27

Be still. Be silent. Be the person you wish to be. Allow space around your 'character'. Mime. Dance. Let your body speak. Mime can express tragedy and transformation. Dance takes both into joy.

28

To 'establish' a 'momentum' is so to give shape to a tradition that it is able to keep moving. It is not to set it in stone, in any one form of 'establishment' that can so easily calcify.

29

For Thomas Aquinas, 'sin' is that which darkens the mind, refusing to recognize the 'blindingly' obvious. Seized by moral blindness, you walk unaware into danger, caught by evil's trap, snare, glare.

30

If you dig deep, reflect long, and act in spiralling patterns of faithful loving, you will be a traditional radical, continually radicalizing the tradition.

31

You will disintegrate into what has no recognizable form, beyond that of dust or bleached bones. Can you let that happen, trusting that the Spirit will as always brood, your dying but a prelude to new life?

NOVEMBER

1

Nicholas Berdyaev said that we are looking for a new kind of saint, for men and women who will take upon themselves the burden of a complex world.

2

Status and wealth shout silently, making such a noise that you cannot hear the whispered cries of those from whose fear your status has been reached and from whose labour your wealth has been acquired.

3

You are loved – accepted – forgiven – cherished: you are of infinite worth. And without you, the rest of us are deprived of all the ways in which you could enrich our lives. *[After Leo Buscaglia, The Parsonage]*

4

Soul-deep, your being rises to meet the landscapes of air and light, of vast horizons, of height and depth, once you have acknowledged their implacable 'thus-ness' which you cannot shape to your own ends.

5

On learning how to eat a meal on your own: flowers, a lit candle, a glass of wine, a carefully set table, and either music or a good book. (And from time to time invite a companion to join you.) *[After May Sarton]*

6

If you are not really with me, you are an empty presence. If you are fully alive, you are a real presence. And when you have left, you are still here.

7

Be professional – skilled, conscientious, accountable – for others' sake. Be an amateur – a lover of the work – for your own sake. Be both, for God's sake.

8

Be stern with yourself to ward off distractions and close the door against intruders. Only then can you dare to be vulnerable enough to be creative: gentle with yourself, you can open your depths to the truth.

9

To be *good* demands a strong will and constant practice. To be *holy* is to know that you can easily still be bad, and to leave the transformation to God. Holiness may creep up on you unawares: it is always a gift.

10

You may not be indispensable, but you are irreplaceable. You are singular, unique and unrepeatable. *And* everyone else is present in you. *And* you flourish only by encounter, exchange and co-inherence.

11

Tuck away your faith in the corners of your life, so hidden that you seem to lose it. Let it do its own work in and through everything you do. And when you speak of it, better not shout, rather whisper.

12

Alone, yet you are a cell of the living organism, even a miniature church, in communion with all the others, bearing in your own being all that is necessary to evoke and receive the Mysterious One.

13

Alone, you need others to avoid being too ec-centric, to be equipped, encouraged and critiqued, and to recognize that you belong to a greater whole, more than the sum of all of us. (And for a party.)

14

'Religion' is practised by those who are afraid of hell. 'Spirituality' is practised by those who know what hell is like. (There may of course be good religion and bad spirituality. As ever, discern.)

15

In the place of burial, of disintegration, there is either nothing at all, or nothing of significance, yet in it and through it there may also be a revelation, the impossible, unexpected gift of transformed life.

16

To be completely still is to be a corpse. Be thankful that you are restless. incomplete. Disturbed, imperfect, you are still being worked on, still on a journey, and there is still more to discover and learn.

17

Do you suffer from the 'haunting' music of a fast-disappearing 'God'? Are you fearful of the silence that descends? Can you wait, trusting that new music will begin to sound, however distant, in your ears?

18

You, or your organization, becomes decadent when you try to maintain, at great expense and great inconvenience, old traditions from which the meaning has departed. *[After Tom Baker]*

19

Let go into the abyss, and trust that you will be seized by the albatross, your pain-wracked arms lifted up and down in the rhythm of wings, charging you with new energy, your pain alive with exultation.

20

Do not become absolutely attached to any one particular form, but love well whatever form you discern as best – or good enough – for the shaping of spirit, for the time being.

21

Your defences, your roles, your possessions, your status, all are facades, at worst totally obscuring your true self, at best caretakers for that soul-deep self, vulnerable, frightened, yearning. *[After John Lee]*

22

Unity is not a static equilibrium, but a dynamic balance, not a single fixed viewpoint but co-inherence at every level of reality, a deep and ultimately unbreakable connection of everything and everyone.

23

Not soul vs. body, or spirit vs. flesh, but surface-self vs. deep-self, superficial-self vs. core-self, false self vs. true self, smoke-self vs. flame-self. *[The last contrast by Thomas Merton]*

24

Bitter hatred, cold-blooded vengeance, eats away inside you, sours relationships, and in destroying leaves but ashes in the mouth. Ask yourself if you are 'harbouring' resentment, giving it safe anchorage.

25

Anger joined with compassion has power to make changes for the good of both. It is a warm energy if the other person matters, if there is at least a level of trust and a constructive intent.

26

In conflict, recognize that the other has concerns that are genuine. Neither can claim to be absolutely right. The cost of reconciliation has to be shared. The resolution lies *beyond* the current position of each.

27

Faced with a fanatic, be clear and consistent and calm. Point out where the logic of the others' attitude leads. Keep a sense of humour. Do not be trapped into giving back in similar kind.

28

Faced with a fanatic, use anger sparingly, never detached from truth and compassion. Tell something of your story, enough to show that you are vulnerable, not enough to be trampled upon.

29

Faced with a fanatic, remember that arguments build up opposing strengths, while stories await a response. Remember that you may not change your opponent but you may well influence the onlookers.

30

To believe is not to assent to propositions or even creeds. It is to cherish someone or something. The word 'belief' comes from the word 'lief', meaning 'to hold dear'.

DECEMBER

1

The divine is a continuously present active verb rather than a static definitive noun. To pray is to be in the present moving presence and to share in continuing personal action.

2

Skin is delicate, sensitive to touch, exquisitely pleasurable, vulnerable to pain. The two most sensitive surfaces of the body can get clap. (The other is the eye.) *[After Eric Griffiths]*

3

If you are unworldly in your religion, you are likely to have more faith in the powers that be than those who engage the world with compassion and justice, who tend to fall foul of the powers that be.

4

Do not cut knots. Patiently disentangle the threads. Pay attention to complexities and contradictions. *Contemplate* the presently unresolvable, content with uncertainty, doubt, mystery. Only then decide and act.

5

Be loyal to what is yet to be. Trust that which does not yet exist. Listen for what has not yet been heard. Look for the as yet unformed image in the piece of wood or the lump of rock.

6

Ask yourself in what ways you were taught to think of yourself as superior and privileged, and in what ways inferior to others, stigmatized and pushed to the margins?

7

To be pushed off the edge is to be expendable, homeless, slave labour, a factory 'hand', dismissable, having no say in your destiny and no power to effect change.

8

Draw near affliction, do not turn away, bring a tentative touch, seek to lessen pain, keep hope alive, do not bury your protest or questions, but patiently probe the dense 'matter' that does not yet yield its meaning.

9

To take off your shoes as you approach the 'holy ground' that is another human being is to remind yourself that the soles of your feet are tender, as is the soul of the one who needs your kindness. *[After Donald Nicholl]*

10

You wish to be free from the encroachment, restraint and tyranny of others. Do not therefore think you are free to impose yourself on others, whether by obvious force or sly insinuation.

11

Mystery is not a puzzle that you can solve but a question that you cannot answer, a reality you can never control, a perplexity that you can only live into.

12

To live into the Mystery is to discover a reality that is supra-personal, the 'under-ground' of your being. That reality wells up within you as pure gift, 'Nothing' to your surface self, 'All' to your deep self.

13

If you live for others so much that you have lost sight of your own needs, you will miss those who long to give to you and long for you to receive. You *are* of worth. Can you not risk opening your hands?

14

To wash up together lightens the load: for the host the chore is shared and becomes enjoyable; for the guest, it is simpler than at home. And your neighbour's shopping bag is always lighter than your own.

15

From your belly comes your infant self, roaring, sobbing, shrieking. Trust the power that your adult self now knows, transforming those wounded sounds, now become growling, rumbling, chuckling.

16

Do you wake up and feed when the clock says so – the *alarm* clock for the *everyday*! Learn to listen to your body. Sleep when you are tired. Eat when you are hungry. Take time to let happen, to let be.

17

If you are totally aware, totally in the present, totally attentive, totally engaged – here, now, today – tomorrow has no power over you, for it neither exists for you nor impinges upon you.

18

A fantasy or a vision? How can you tell? Ask these questions: Does it imply chores? Can it be embodied? Will it cost? Does it involve your imagination? Are others potentially involved? Does it feel solid?

19

If you have no surface energy, recognize that your *reserve* energy is depleted, as a *reservoir* after a dry summer. Slow down, return to your sources of renewal, wait for the flow – in its own time.

20

Words well crafted can create a temporary sacred space for truth, compassion, light, meaning, protected from the encroaching falsehoods, cruelty, darkness, disintegration.

21

But do not let yourself be spell-bound, en-chanted, en-tranced by the verbal magicians. There is a power to corrupt, to bewitch, to spread evil. The power of words at religious and political rallies?

22

Be jolted out of any complacency that you possess the truth, the Word, *against* all others. Respond rather to the challenge to live the truth, the Word, *towards communion with* all others.

23

Beware honorifics, status, pedestals, podiums, eloquence, well-crafted set pieces, speakers with scripts written for them, fingers that point – especially if they are well manicured.

24

Hold to the image of the sculpture of the Mother and Child where the Mother is smiling in contentment and the Child on her lap chuckling. Why is so much art with religious themes so *solemn*?

25

A baby, eyes closed, sleeps serenely. A baby, eyes opened, looks with wonder. Such is the birthright of the twice-newly-born. May such a Christ-child be born in us today.

26

Jesus was shamed and dishonoured. The early Church wrote of his being buried in a rich man's tomb and exalted to a seat at God's right hand. Has such a picture of worldly honour influenced us too much?

27

Jesus applauded his people's enemies – the Samaritan, the Centurion – and put family second. The early Church soon claimed to be law-abiding and no threat to the Emperor.

28

Jesus placed nobodies at the centre of God's domain, as a slave woman washing feet. The early Church adopted hierarchies of power and control, eventually sitting down with the Emperor.

29

Do not be confused: elaborate when necessary, but be lucid. Do not be complicated: honour complexity, but be simple. Do not be opaque: be as profound as you need to be, but be clear.

30

What punctuation mark signals your view of the future, into and beyond the new year? Full stop? Semi-colon? Question mark? Exclamation mark?

31

On this day in 1900 Thomas Hardy heard a thrush defying the desolate winter landscape, its song seeming to be one of trembling hope, of which the bird knew, but of which he was unaware . . .

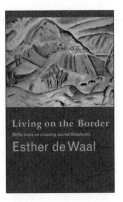